Gooseberry Patch

Christmas Kitchen

Gooseberry Patch

An imprint of Globe Pequot
64 South Main Street
Essex, CT 06426

www.gooseberrypatch.com

1•800•854•6673

Copyright 2023, Gooseberry Patch 978-1-62093-528-6
Photo Edition is a major revision of **Christmas Kitchen**.

Do you have a tried & true recipe...

tip, craft or memory that you'd like to see featured in
a **Gooseberry Patch** cookbook? Visit our website at
www.gooseberrypatch.com and follow the
easy steps to submit your favorite family recipe.

Or send them to us at:

Gooseberry Patch
PO Box 812
Columbus, OH 43216-0812

Don't forget to include the number of servings your recipe
makes, plus your name, address, phone number and
email address. If we select your recipe, your name will
appear right along with it...and you'll receive
a **FREE** copy of the book!

Contents

Dedication

To our family & friends, we wish you a sweet old-fashioned Christmas filled with joy...and homemade cookies & hot cocoa.

Appreciation

Thanks for sharing your cherished recipes and sweet memories...may your days be merry & bright!

Food
for Family
& Friends

Bacon-Cheddar Cheese Ball

Jeannette Hirschberg
Santa Barbara, CA

This tasty cheese ball turns any occasion into a party!

6 slices bacon, crisply cooked
   and crumbled
2 8-oz. pkgs. cream cheese,
   softened
8-oz. pkg. shredded sharp
   Cheddar cheese

1/2 c. green onion, chopped
1 clove garlic, minced
3 T. pimento, diced
3 T. fresh parsley, minced
assorted crackers

Combine all ingredients except crackers, blending well. Form into a ball; cover with plastic wrap. Refrigerate overnight to allow flavors to blend. Serve with crackers. Makes 8 servings.

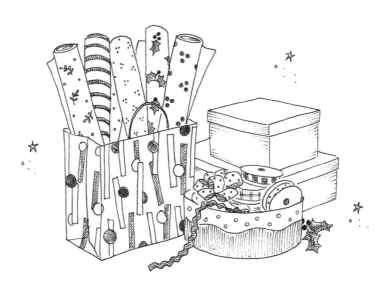

Shopping, wrapping and decorating needn't keep you from getting together with friends at Christmas! Invite them over for appetizers...the recipes are quick & easy to prepare, so more time can be spent enjoying each other's company.

Food for Family & Friends

Mollie's Spinach-Avocado Dip

Mollie Wong
Houston, TX

*My spinach patch is so abundant that a co-worker suggested that
I make some spinach dip and bring it to work for everyone to taste.
After much trial & error, I am pleased to present this final version.
It's scrumptious served with a veggie tray, a jumbo shrimp ring,
crackers or garlic toasts.*

1 lb. baby spinach, coarsely
    chopped
8-oz. can water chestnuts,
    drained and coarsely chopped
3 avocados, pitted, peeled and
    coarsely chopped
3 pickled jalapeños, coarsely
    chopped

1/2 onion, finely chopped
1/2 red pepper, finely chopped
2 cloves garlic, finely chopped
16-oz. container sour cream
2-oz. pkg. vegetable soup mix

In a large bowl, blend all ingredients together. Cover and chill at least
2 hours before serving. Serves 8.

Cut out bite-size pieces of fresh red and yellow pepper
with a star-shaped mini cookie cutter...what a
clever way to trim a veggie dip platter!

Ham & Veggie Crescent Wreath

Sophia Graves
Okeechobee, FL

I made this recipe for my office's Goodie Day and it lasted all of 20 minutes! Everyone that tasted this dish asked for the recipe... it is awesome. It's already on the list for next year's Goodie Day.

2 8-oz. tubes refrigerated
  crescent rolls
8-oz. container pineapple cream
  cheese spread, softened
1/3 c. cooked ham, chopped
1/4 c. yellow pepper, chopped

1/4 c. green pepper, chopped
1/2 c. broccoli flowerets,
  chopped
1 T. red onion, chopped
6 cherry tomatoes, quartered

Turn a 10-ounce custard cup or a small bowl upside-down in the center of an ungreased baking sheet. Remove dough from one tube; do not unroll (keep remaining tube refrigerated). Roll dough between your hands to make a 12-inch log. Cut log into 20 slices. Arrange 16 slices around cup or bowl, slightly overlapping and in a clockwise direction. Roll second tube of dough into a 12-inch log, cutting log into 20 slices. Using 4 slices from first tube and 20 slices from second tube, arrange in a counter-clockwise direction, close to but not overlapping first ring. Remove cup or bowl. Bake at 375 degrees for 15 to 18 minutes, or until lightly golden. Gently loosen wreath from baking sheet; carefully slide onto a wire rack. Cool completely, about 30 minutes. Place wreath on a serving tray or platter. Spread cream cheese over wreath; sprinkle with remaining ingredients. Slice into serving-size pieces. Serve immediately or cover and refrigerate up to 4 hours before serving. Makes 14 to 16 servings.

Food for Family & Friends

Brie Kisses

Kathy Grashoff
Fort Wayne, IN

*I love to make these beautiful appetizers at Christmastime
or on Valentine's Day.*

2/3 lb. Brie cheese   red and/or green hot pepper jelly
17.3-oz. pkg. frozen puff pastry

Cut Brie into 32 1/2-inch cubes; arrange on a plate and place in the
freezer. Let pastry thaw at room temperature 30 minutes; unfold each
pastry and roll with a rolling pin to remove creases. Slice each sheet
into quarters; slice each quarter in half. Cut each piece in half one
more time for a total of 32 squares. Place squares into greased mini
muffin cups; arrange so corners of dough point upward. Bake at
400 degrees for 5 minutes. Place one Brie cube in center of each
pastry. Bake 10 minutes or until edges are golden. Remove from
pan. Immediately top with colorful pepper jelly. Makes 32.

Serve some toasty baguette chips with your favorite holiday
cheese ball. Thinly slice a loaf or baguette of French bread.
Arrange slices on a baking sheet and spray lightly with
non-stick olive oil spray. Bake at 350 degrees for 10 minutes,
or until crunchy and golden.

Peppermint Punch

Christi Ross
Grundy Center, IA

This is my husband's grandmother's recipe. A former restaurant owner, Grandma Ross was known far and wide for this festive and tasty punch. Pink and fluffy, it has been a family favorite for several decades.

1 qt. peppermint ice cream, softened
1 c. milk

2-ltr. bottle ginger ale, chilled
Garnish: whole or finely crushed peppermint sticks

In a large punch bowl, blend together ice cream and milk; stir gently. Slowly add ginger ale; stir until combined. Serve with peppermint stick stirrers or sprinkle with finely crushed candy. Serves 8 to 10.

Evaleah's Christmas Punch

Tawnya McVicker
Hartford City, IN

In our family this punch is so popular that we always have to make two bowls! I'm the third generation to make this punch for our celebrations.

1 gal. lime sherbet
2-ltr. bottle ginger ale, chilled

2-ltr. bottle lemon-lime soda, chilled

Scoop sherbet into a punch bowl; slowly pour sodas over the sherbet. Allow sherbet to melt slightly while mixing gently. Makes 35 to 40 servings.

Festive ice cubes! Drop a couple of cranberries and a sprig of mint into each section of an ice cube tray. Fill with distilled water for crystal-clear cubes and freeze.

Food for Family & Friends

Spiced Christmas Cashews

Paula Marchesi
Lenhartsville, PA

These well-seasoned cashews are sweet, salty and crunchy...and oh-so snackable! Everybody raves about them. I often make 10 to 12 batches for gifts during the holiday season...maybe even more!

1 egg white	1 T. chili powder
1 T. water	2 t. salt
2 9-3/4 oz. cans salted cashews	2 t. ground cumin
1/3 c. sugar	1/2 t. cayenne pepper

Whisk together egg white and water in a large bowl. Add cashews; toss to coat. Transfer to a colander; drain for 2 minutes. In a separate bowl, combine sugar and spices; add cashews and toss to coat. Arrange in a single layer on a greased 15"x10" jelly-roll pan. Bake, uncovered, at 250 degrees for 50 to 55 minutes, stirring once. Cool on a wire rack. Store in an airtight container. Makes about 3-1/2 cups.

Feathery flakes are falling, falling
From the skies in the softest way,
And between are voices calling,
"Soon it will be Christmas Day!"
– Mary B. Dodge

Vicki's Spaghetti Sauce

Vicki Holt
Valley View, TX

This homemade sauce is oh-so fast, easy and good...perfect for sharing with family & friends! It also freezes really well. A mix of seasoned and plain canned tomatoes results in really good flavor with little extra effort.

1 lb. ground beef
19.76-oz. pkg. sweet or spicy
   Italian pork sausages,
   casings removed
1 onion, chopped
3 cloves garlic, chopped
Optional: 1/2 lb. sliced
   mushrooms
2 14-1/2 oz. cans diced
   tomatoes with basil,
   garlic & oregano
14-1/2 oz. can diced tomatoes
3 6-oz. cans tomato paste with
   basil, garlic & oregano

3 8-oz. cans tomato sauce with
   basil, garlic & oregano
15-oz. can tomato sauce
3/4 c. water
1/4 c. dried parsley
salt and pepper
1 T. brown sugar, packed
Optional: red pepper flakes
   to taste
1/2 c. grated Parmesan cheese
cooked pasta

In a large stockpot over medium heat, brown ground beef and sausages; drain. Add onion, garlic and mushrooms, if using; cook for 5 minutes. Add remaining ingredients except pasta. Reduce heat; simmer for 30 minutes, stirring occasionally. Serve over cooked pasta. Serves 8 to 10.

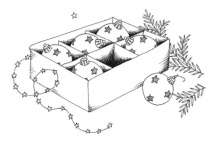

Trimming the tree is such fun with friends. Put a big pot of Vicki's Spaghetti Sauce on to simmer...when the last strand of tinsel is hung, dinner will be ready!

Food for Family & Friends

Great-Aunt Georgia's Lasagna

Jill Adams
Bakersfield, CA

My mother made this lasagna all the time when I was growing up.
We always had it for Christmas dinner because it's easy to make ahead
and refrigerate, then reheat. Now I do the same with my own family.

19.76-oz. pkg. sweet or spicy
    Italian pork sausages,
    casings removed
3 6-oz. cans tomato paste
2-1/4 c. water
3 T. spaghetti sauce mix
1/4 c. olive oil
3/4 c. red wine vinegar
15-oz. can black olives, drained
    and sliced

16-oz. pkg. lasagna noodles,
    cooked
16-oz. container cottage or
    ricotta cheese
1 c. grated Parmesan cheese
8-oz. pkg. shredded mozzarella
    cheese

In a large pot over medium heat, brown sausages until crumbly. Drain
on paper towels. Stir tomato paste into drippings in same pot. Add
water, sauce mix, oil and vinegar; mix well and simmer for 15 to
20 minutes. Add sausages and olives; heat through. Spray a
13"x9" baking pan with non-stick vegetable spray. Arrange in
3 layers, as follows: 4 lasagna noodles, 1/3 of sauce, 1/3 of cottage or
ricotta and Parmesan cheeses, ending with Parmesan cheese on top.
Bake, uncovered, at 350 degrees for 30 minutes, or until hot and
bubbly. Let stand for 10 minutes; cut into squares. Can be made
ahead of time and refrigerated or frozen. Serves 10 to 12.

Make-ahead casseroles
are perfect for family meals
after a day of Christmas
shopping. For an easy side,
whip up a marinated salad
to keep in the fridge...cut up
crunchy veggies and toss with
zesty Italian salad dressing.

Chicken, Spinach & Bows Casserole
Karen Fulton
Huntington, IN

Adapted from a recipe that was my grandmother's. It feeds a lot of people, so it was great for our last family reunion!

16-oz. pkg. bowtie pasta, cooked
26-oz. can cream of chicken soup
16-oz. pkg. frozen chopped spinach, thawed
4 to 5 boneless, skinless chicken breasts, cooked and diced

8-oz. pkg. shredded Colby-Jack cheese
1 T. butter, sliced
salt and pepper to taste

Combine cooked pasta and soup; stir until coated. Add spinach and set aside. In a lightly greased 3-quart glass casserole dish, layer half each of chicken, pasta mixture and cheese. Layer with remaining chicken and pasta mixture; dot with butter and sprinkle with remaining cheese. Bake, covered, at 350 degrees for 30 to 45 minutes, until heated through and cheese is melted. Serves 10 to 15.

Placecards make any holiday meal special. For a clever holder, simply hot-glue three candy canes together to make an easel.

Food for Family & Friends

Mozzarella, Sausage & Pasta

Emily Regier
Kingman, KS

Whip up this tasty casserole to pop in the oven after returning from a family sledding party! By the time wet socks and mittens have been pulled off, you'll have a hot, hearty dinner everyone will love.

1 lb. ground mild Italian pork
    sausage
2 T. butter
3 T. all-purpose flour
1 t. salt
1/2 t. pepper

2 c. milk
3/4 c. grated Parmesan cheese
1 c. shredded mozzarella
    cheese, divided
12-oz. pkg. bowtie pasta,
    cooked

Brown sausage in a large skillet over medium heat. Drain and set aside. Melt butter in skillet; stir in flour, salt and pepper. Gradually add milk; cook and stir until thickened. Remove from heat; add Parmesan cheese and 1/2 cup mozzarella cheese. Stir until blended; mix in cooked pasta and sausage. Spoon into a greased 2-quart casserole dish and bake, uncovered, for 20 minutes at 350 degrees. Sprinkle with remaining mozzarella; bake for an additional 5 minutes. Serves 6.

Start a new family tradition...a holiday journal to record sweet and funny moments together. Older kids might like to write stories or take snapshots, while young children can add crayon drawings. Every year, bring out the journal to read past entries and add new ones. Memories in the making!

That Broccoli Casserole

Debra Elliott
Danville, VA

Eggs, mushrooms and cheese crackers really jazz up this winner of a recipe! I jotted it down from a magazine at least 10 years ago. I'm asked to bring this dish to every church potluck...the pan always goes home empty.

2 10-3/4 oz. cans cream of
   celery soup
1 c. mayonnaise
8-oz. container sour cream
2 T. lemon juice
1 t. pepper
10-oz. pkg. baked cheese
   crackers, crushed
1/4 c. butter, melted

32-oz. pkg. frozen broccoli,
   cooked and drained
6 eggs, hard-boiled, peeled
   and sliced
8-oz. can sliced mushrooms,
   drained
8-oz. pkg. shredded Cheddar
   cheese

Blend together soup, mayonnaise, sour cream, lemon juice and pepper; set aside. Sprinkle crushed crackers into a lightly greased 13"x9" baking pan; drizzle with butter. Spoon half the soup mixture over cracker crumbs; arrange broccoli over soup mixture. Arrange sliced eggs over broccoli; sprinkle with mushrooms. Spoon remaining soup mixture over top; sprinkle with cheese. Bake, uncovered, at 400 degrees for about 30 minutes, or until hot and bubbly. Serves 10 to 12.

A countertop mug tree makes a fun display rack for cherished Christmas ornaments.

Food for Family & Friends

Creamy Potatoes Au Gratin

Tami Bowman
Marysville, OH

Hearty and comforting...everyone's favorite.

4 russet potatoes, peeled, sliced
    1/4-inch thick and divided
1 onion, thinly sliced
salt and pepper to taste
3 T. butter

3 T. all-purpose flour
1/2 t. salt
2 c. milk
1-1/2 c. shredded Cheddar
    cheese

Arrange half of potato slices in a greased one-quart casserole dish. Top with onion and remaining potatoes; add salt and pepper to taste. In a medium saucepan, melt butter over medium heat. Add flour and salt; stir constantly with a whisk for one minute. Stir in milk; cook until thickened. Stir in cheese; continue to stir until melted. Pour cheese sauce over potatoes; cover with aluminum foil. Bake at 400 degrees for 1-1/2 hours. Serves 4.

With houses decorated inside and out for the holidays, it's a great time to hold a progressive dinner! Each family serves one course at their house as everyone travels from home to home. Begin at one house for appetizers, move to the next for soups and salads, again for the main dish and end with dessert. It's all about food & fun!

Swiss Steak Stew

Debbie Deverill
Gilbert, AZ

This satisfying slow-cooker stew is easy to prepare. As it cooks,
your whole house smells just wonderful too!

1/4 c. all-purpose flour
1/2 t. salt
1-1/2 lbs. beef round steak,
   cut into bite-size pieces
3 c. new red potatoes, peeled
   and quartered
1 onion, diced
1 clove garlic, minced

14-1/2 oz. can Italian-style
   diced tomatoes
3/4 c. beef broth or water
1 c. canned sliced carrots
1 c. canned corn
1 c. canned green beans

Mix flour and salt together in a shallow bowl. Add beef; toss to coat
well. Spray a skillet with non-stick vegetable spray; heat over medium
heat. Brown beef on all sides. In a slow cooker, layer potatoes, beef,
onion and garlic. Stir together tomatoes, broth or water and any
remaining flour mixture; pour over top. Cover and cook on low setting
for 7 to 8 hours, until beef is tender. Add remaining vegetables
and cook until warmed through, about 10 to 15 minutes. Makes
6 servings.

Make a savory meal even better! Serve up Swiss Steak Stew
in hollowed-out round loaves of crusty bread...
so cozy shared in front of a crackling fire.

Food for Family & Friends

Biscuit Dinner

Debra Manley
Bowling Green, OH

This dish is pure comfort...it really hits the spot on a chilly evening.

1 lb. ground beef
1/2 c. onion, chopped
1/2 t. dried thyme
1/2 t. paprika
1/4 t. pepper

14-oz. can beef broth, divided
1/3 c. all-purpose flour
10-oz. pkg. frozen mixed
  vegetables, thawed
12-oz. tube refrigerated biscuits

Brown beef in a large skillet over medium heat; drain. Add onion and seasonings; cook until meat is browned and onion is translucent. Combine 1/4 cup broth with flour; stir until smooth and set aside. Add remaining broth to meat mixture in skillet; bring to a boil. Gradually add flour mixture, stirring constantly until smooth; simmer for 5 minutes. Add vegetables; cook for an additional 2 to 3 minutes. Transfer to a lightly greased 1-1/2 quart casserole dish; top with biscuits. Bake, uncovered, at 375 degrees for 25 to 30 minutes, until biscuits are golden. Serves 4 to 6.

Place newly arrived Christmas cards in a vintage napkin holder, then take a moment every evening to share happy holiday greetings from friends & neighbors over dinner!

Chicken & Artichoke Bake

Joann Drake
Pioneer, CA

*An all-time favorite recipe that I have given out many times to
friends & family...it belonged to my grandmother whom
I especially loved and miss.*

2 9-oz. pkgs. frozen artichokes
2 t. olive oil
2 cloves garlic, minced
3 c. cooked chicken, cubed
2 10-3/4 oz. cans cream of
  chicken soup
1/2 c. mayonnaise

1 t. lemon juice
1 t. curry powder
1-1/4 c. shredded sharp
  Cheddar cheese
1-1/4 c. soft bread crumbs
2 T. melted butter

Cook artichokes according to package directions, adding oil and
garlic to cooking water. Drain artichokes and arrange in a greased
13"x9" baking pan. Spread chicken over artichokes. Combine soup,
mayonnaise, lemon juice and curry powder; mix well and pour over
chicken. Sprinkle with cheese. Toss bread crumbs in melted butter
to coat; sprinkle over cheese. Bake, uncovered, at 350 degrees for
25 minutes. Makes 8 servings.

Set a pine-scented potted rosemary wreath in a kitchen
window...oh-so handy for adding flavorful fresh sprigs to
roasting meats and vegetables. Tie on tiny red bows to
contrast with the evergreen foliage...delightful!

Food for Family & Friends

Tangy Chicken Piccata

A.M. Gilstrap
Easley, SC

*A family favorite that's worthy of a holiday meal! Serve with
a savory rice pilaf and a fresh spinach salad.*

1 lb. boneless, skinless chicken
    breasts
2 T. all-purpose flour
1 T. oil
1/2 c. orange juice

1/4 c. orange marmalade
1/4 c. honey mustard
1/4 t. dried rosemary
1 orange, peeled, quartered and
    thinly sliced

Dredge chicken in flour; set aside. Heat oil in a large cast-iron skillet
over medium heat. Add chicken and cook for 5 minutes, or until
golden on both sides. Add orange juice, marmalade, mustard and
rosemary; bring to a boil. Reduce heat to low. Simmer for 5 minutes,
or until chicken juices run clear. Stir in orange slices and heat through.
Serves 4.

After a hearty meal, enjoy a frosty walk around the
neighborhood to enjoy the twinkling Christmas lights.

Cheesy Corn & Pasta Bake

Anna Taylor
Muncie, IN

We just love this fix & forget recipe...it tosses together in a snap!

16-oz. can corn, drained
16-oz. can creamed corn
1 c. pasteurized process cheese
   spread, cubed
1 c. butter, melted

1/2 to 1 c. milk
1 T. dried, minced onion
8-oz. pkg. spaghetti, uncooked
   and broken into 1-inch
   lengths

Combine all ingredients in a slow cooker; stir until well mixed. Cover and cook on high setting for 2 hours. Stir once and cover again. Reduce heat to low setting; cook for an additional 2 hours. Makes 6 to 8 servings.

Corn Custard Mexicana

Judy Lillemoen
Santa Ana, CA

I've been serving up this warm, comforting side dish ever since
a friend shared it with me nearly 40 years ago.

2 c. frozen corn, thawed
2 eggs, beaten
1 c. sour cream
1/2 c. yellow cornmeal
1 t. salt

1 T. chopped pimento
2 T. celery, chopped
4-oz. can diced green chiles
1 c. Monterey Jack cheese, diced
Optional: 1/2 c. butter, melted

Mix all ingredients in a large bowl. Pour into a buttered 1-1/2 quart casserole dish. Bake, covered, at 350 degrees for 45 to 50 minutes, until golden and set. Serves 6 to 8.

God bless us, every one!
– Charles Dickens

Food for Family & Friends

Marie's Yeast Rolls

Marie Stewart
Pensacola, FL

After playing with grandchildren all day, who has time to knead and roll wonderful rolls that taste just like bakery rolls? This batter can be refrigerated in an airtight container up to 2 weeks...so convenient!

1 env. active dry yeast
2 c. warm water
1/2 c. margarine, melted

1/4 c. sugar
1 egg, beaten
4 c. self-rising flour

Dissolve yeast in warm water, about 110 to 115 degrees. Mix all ingredients together and stir well. Put a heaping tablespoon into well greased muffin cups. Bake at 425 degrees for 20 minutes, or until golden. Makes 3 dozen.

Quick Cheese Bread

Lisa Ashton
Aston, PA

My kids just love to spread this bread with lots of butter! It reheats well in the microwave too.

2 c. biscuit baking mix
1-1/2 c. shredded Cheddar
   cheese, divided

2 eggs, beaten
3/4 c. milk
2 T. butter, diced

Combine baking mix and one cup cheese. Whisk eggs with milk and mix with dry ingredients; mix well. Turn batter out into a well greased 9"x5" loaf pan. Dot with butter and sprinkle with remaining cheese. Bake at 350 degrees for 45 minutes. Let cool completely. Makes one loaf.

Slip a terra cotta warming tile into a napkin-lined
basket of freshly baked bread to keep it
warm and tasty all through dinner.

Sausage Noodle Stew

Julie Russell
Delaware, OH

Sprinkle with freshly shredded Parmesan cheese for even more flavor.

1 lb. ground Italian pork
   sausage
2 14-1/2 oz. cans Italian-style
   diced tomatoes
15-oz. can kidney beans,
   drained and rinsed
2 14-1/2 oz. cans beef broth

1 c. water
1/2 t. dried oregano
12-oz. pkg. frozen homestyle
   egg noodles
16-oz. pkg. frozen Italian-blend
   vegetables

Brown sausage in a Dutch oven over medium heat; drain. Add tomatoes, beans, broth, water and oregano; bring to a boil. Add frozen noodles; simmer for 20 minutes. Add frozen vegetables and cook for an additional 5 to 10 minutes, until noodles are done. Makes 4 to 6 servings.

For a quick & easy mantel decoration, spell out "Merry Christmas" with vintage alphabet blocks.

Food for Family & Friends

Country-Style Chicken Pie

Ann Bolick
Plano, TX

My always-hungry teens beg me for this hearty two-crust pie.

2 to 3 boneless, skinless
    chicken breasts, cooked
    and diced
1 c. broccoli, chopped
4-oz. can sliced mushrooms,
    drained
3/4 c. frozen corn
1/4 c. onion, chopped
1/3 c. frozen shredded
    hashbrowns

10-3/4 oz. can cream of
    mushroom soup
1/4 c. sour cream
1/3 c. plus 1 t. milk, divided
salt and pepper to taste
2 9-inch pie crusts
1 egg white
garlic salt to taste

Mix chicken and vegetables in a large bowl; set aside. In a small bowl, mix together soup, sour cream, 1/3 cup milk, salt and pepper; stir into chicken mixture. Spread in a pie crust; top with second pie crust. Seal, flute and vent top crust. Whisk together egg white and remaining milk; brush over crust. Sprinkle lightly with garlic salt. Wrap a thin strip of aluminum foil around edge of crust to prevent browning. Bake at 375 degrees for 40 minutes. Let stand for 5 minutes before slicing. Serves 6.

Be sure to share family tales at Christmastime...they're super conversation starters. How about the time Grandma set out cookies to cool and Skippy the dog ate them, or the year a big snowstorm led to a houseful of extra Christmas guests... it's such fun to share stories like these!

Stuffed Ham & Swiss Rolls

Linda Belon
Wintersville, OH

Serve with steamed asparagus and parsley new potatoes...a dinner that's good enough for guests, yet ready to serve in just minutes.

2 c. herb-flavored stuffing cubes
1/2 c. boiling water
2 T. plus 2 t. margarine, divided
8 slices deli ham

8 slices Swiss cheese
1 egg, beaten
1 T. water
1/2 c. dry bread crumbs

Combine stuffing, boiling water and 2 tablespoons margarine. Cover and let stand for 5 minutes. Top each ham slice with a cheese slice. Spoon 1/4 cup stuffing mixture over center of cheese; roll up and secure with a toothpick. Whisk egg and water together. Roll ham rolls in egg mixture, then roll in bread crumbs. In a large skillet over medium heat, sauté ham rolls in remaining margarine for 4 to 5 minutes, or until golden, turning only once. Discard toothpicks before serving. Serves 4.

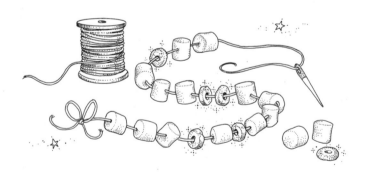

Using mini marshmallows, sturdy thread and a blunt needle, children will have fun making garlands to wind around the Christmas tree...it's much easier for little hands than stringing popcorn.

Food for Family & Friends

Beef-Broccoli Wellington

Cindy Kerekes
Wharton, NJ

We love this quick take on an old favorite.

1-1/2 lbs. ground beef
1 onion, chopped
6-1/2 oz. can mushroom stems
   and pieces, drained
20-oz. pkg. frozen chopped
   broccoli, thawed

1 lb. shredded mozzarella
   cheese
8-oz. container sour cream
2 8-oz. tubes refrigerated
   crescent rolls

In a skillet over medium heat, brown ground beef with onion and mushrooms; drain. Stir in broccoli and cheese. When cheese is melted, stir in sour cream. Line a lightly greased 13"x9" pan with one tube crescent rolls. Spoon ground beef mixture over rolls; arrange remaining rolls on top. Bake, uncovered, at 350 degrees for 15 minutes, or until golden. Cut into squares to serve. Makes 6 servings.

An advent calendar helps the days pass for eager kids! Create your own with pictures clipped from old Christmas cards... behind each door, write a quick fun-to-do idea, like "Make a paper chain" or "Feed the birds" or "Write a letter to Santa." Open each door at breakfast to share the day's activity together.

Grandma's Christmas Eve Casserole
Amy Nelson
Lolo, MT

When I was growing up, we would spend every Christmas Eve at my Grandma Sjostrom's house. Every year she made this casserole for dinner...its aroma while baking takes me right back to when I was a little girl. She has since passed on, but I continue to make it on Christmas Eve for my own family. It is simple, satisfying and feeds an army!

1/2 c. butter
1 lb. ground beef
1 lb. ground pork
1 c. green pepper, chopped
1 c. celery, chopped
2 c. onion, chopped
1/3 c. chopped black olives
2 4-oz. cans sliced mushrooms,
    drained and liquid from 1 can
    reserved

2 t. salt
10-3/4 oz. can tomato soup
2 8-oz. cans tomato sauce
16-oz. pkg. curly egg noodles,
    cooked
8-oz. pkg. shredded Cheddar
    cheese

Melt butter in a large skillet over medium heat. Add meat and vegetables; sprinkle with salt. Cook until meat is browned and vegetables are tender; drain. Stir in soup and sauce; simmer for 5 minutes. Stir together soup mixture and cooked noodles; place in a lightly greased 13"x9" baking pan. Sprinkle cheese on top and bake, uncovered, at 350 degrees for 35 minutes. Serves 8 to 10.

Having an informal party during the holidays? Keep it simple...make one or two easy dishes and just pick up tasty go-withs like deli salads, pickles, snack crackers and cocktail nuts at a neighborhood grocery store.

Food for Family & Friends

Baked Kielbasa & Sauerkraut

Melissa Hurbanek
Newburgh, NY

A hearty, filling meal-in-one...just the thing for a busy shopping day!

5 slices bacon, chopped and
  crisply cooked
14-oz. pkg. Kielbasa, sliced
  into bite-size pieces
16-oz. can sauerkraut, drained

16-oz. can whole tomatoes,
  chopped
1/2 c. onion, chopped
3/4 c. brown sugar, packed
hot pepper sauce to taste

Mix all ingredients together. Spread into a lightly greased
13"x9" baking pan. Bake, covered, at 350 degrees for one hour.
Serves 6 to 8.

For frosty fun, layer white paper snowflake cut-outs
between clear glass plates.

Hearty Cheese & Shells

Charish Paul
Dayton, OH

*This casserole is delicious, filling and can be assembled
in a few minutes...a perfect potluck dish!*

2 lbs. ground beef
1 T. oil
2 onions, chopped
1 clove garlic, pressed
14-oz. jar spaghetti sauce
15-oz. can stewed tomatoes

3-oz. jar sliced mushrooms
8-oz. pkg. shell pasta, cooked
3 c. sour cream
1/2 lb. sliced provolone cheese
1/2 lb. sliced mozzarella cheese

In a large, deep skillet over medium heat, brown ground beef in oil, stirring often; drain. Add onions, garlic, sauce, tomatoes and undrained mushrooms; mix well. Simmer for 20 minutes. In a lightly greased deep 3-quart casserole dish, layer half of cooked shells, half of ground beef mixture and half of sour cream; top with provolone cheese. Layer with remaining shells, ground beef mixture and sour cream; top with mozzarella cheese. Cover; bake at 350 degrees for 35 minutes. Uncover and bake for 10 minutes, until cheese melts and is slightly golden. Makes 12 servings.

Do you love the golden glow of candlelight, but worry
about an open flame? Tuck battery-operated tealights
and pillars into favorite votives, sconces and
centerpieces for a safe, soft glow.

Food for Family & Friends

Chicken & Cauliflower

Wendy Lee Paffenroth
Pine Island, NY

With a crisp green salad and a basket of warm biscuits,
this becomes a complete meal.

1 head cauliflower, cut into
   bite-size flowerets
1 bunch broccoli, cut into
   bite-size flowerets
1-1/2 lbs. boneless, skinless
   chicken breasts, cooked
   and cubed

16-oz. pkg. wide egg noodles,
   cooked
2 10-3/4 oz. cans Cheddar
   cheese soup
1-1/2 c. milk
1 T. dried chives
pepper and paprika to taste

Bring a large saucepan of water to boil over medium-high heat; add
cauliflower and broccoli. Cook until crisp-tender, about 2 to 3 minutes;
drain. Toss together chicken, vegetables and cooked noodles in a
lightly greased 13"x9" baking pan; set aside. Combine soup and milk
in a medium saucepan over low heat. Stir together until smooth and
beginning to simmer; pour over top and mix well. Sprinkle with
chives, pepper and paprika. Bake, uncovered, at 325 degrees for
about 30 minutes, until hot and bubbly. Serves 6 to 8.

For the prettiest placecards, spray pinecones gold
with metallic craft paint and tuck in a card
with each guest's name.

Baked Ziti Supreme

Andrea Woodard
Lafayette, TN

*Substitute curly rotini for the ziti, if you like...add ripe olives
or mushrooms. Come and get it!*

1 lb. ground beef
28-oz. jar spaghetti sauce
8-oz. pkg. shredded mozzarella
    cheese, divided

8-oz. pkg. ziti pasta, cooked
1/4 c. grated Parmesan cheese

Brown ground beef in a large saucepan over medium-high heat; drain.
Sir in sauce, one cup mozzarella cheese and cooked pasta. Spoon
into a lightly greased shallow 3-quart casserole dish; sprinkle with
remaining mozzarella and Parmesan cheese. Bake, covered, at
350 degrees for 30 minutes, until hot and bubbly. Serves 6.

For an easy beginning to a savory meal, set out a piping-
hot loaf of Italian bread and a little dish of olive oil
sprinkled with Italian seasoning for dipping.

Food for Family & Friends

Sausage & 3-Pepper Penne

Lorrie Haskell
Lyndeborough, NH

*If you like county fair sausage & pepper sandwiches,
you'll really go for this quick-to-fix skillet meal.*

19.76-oz. pkg. hot Italian
    pork sausages, sliced into
    1-inch pieces
1 green pepper, diced
1 red pepper, diced
1 yellow pepper, diced
1/2 c. onion, chopped
2 cloves garlic, minced

14-oz. can diced tomatoes
8-oz. can tomato sauce
2 t. Italian seasoning
8-oz. pkg. penne pasta, cooked
1/4 c. grated Parmesan cheese

Cook sausages in a skillet over medium-high heat until browned.
Remove sausage from skillet and set aside. In same skillet, cook
pepper, onion and garlic in sausage drippings until peppers are
crisp-tender. Stir in tomatoes, sauce, seasoning and cooked sausages.
Simmer for another one to 2 minutes, until heated through. Pour
sauce over cooked pasta; mix thoroughly. Top with Parmesan cheese.
Makes 6 servings.

Have an appetizer swap with 3 or 4 girlfriends! Each makes
a big batch of her favorite dip, spread or finger food, then
get together to sample and divide 'em up. You'll all have
a super variety of goodies for holiday parties.

Cheesy Potato Puffs

Barb Sulser
Delaware, OH

We can't stop eating these golden puffs!

4-oz. pkg. instant mashed
  potatoes

1/2 c. shredded Cheddar cheese
1/2 c. bacon bits

Prepare instant potatoes according to package directions; let cool. Stir in cheese; roll into 1-1/2 inch balls. Roll balls in bacon bits; arrange on an ungreased baking sheet. Bake at 375 degrees for 15 to 18 minutes. Serves 4.

White Bean &
Tomato Salad
15 oz. can cannellini or
  navy beans, drained
  and rinsed
3 T. olive oil
2 T lemon juice
1/4 c. fresh cilantro

For a gift they'll "flip" over, copy tried & true recipes onto 4"x6" index cards and slip into a flip photo album.

Food for Family & Friends

Buffalo Potato Wedges

Victoria Francis
McHenry, IL

Irresistible as either a side dish or an appetizer.

6 to 8 potatoes, sliced into
   wedges
1 to 2 T. olive oil
salt, pepper and garlic powder
   to taste

1/4 c. butter
1/2 c. hot pepper sauce
Optional: blue cheese salad
   dressing

Arrange potato wedges on a baking sheet sprayed with non-stick vegetable spray. Drizzle with oil; sprinkle with salt, pepper and garlic powder. Bake at 375 degrees for about 30 minutes until tender, tossing occasionally. Remove pan from oven. Combine butter and hot sauce in a microwave-safe bowl. Microwave on high setting until melted, one minute or so; mix well. Drizzle mixture over potato wedges; return to oven for an additional 15 minutes. If desired, serve with salad dressing for dipping. Serves 8 to 10.

Serve up a festive sandwich buffet for an oh-so-easy gathering. Set out a savory selection of deli meats, cheeses, breads and other fixin's for make-your-own-sandwiches... even gourmet mustards. Add a tabletop grill for making hot sandwiches, then just relax and enjoy your guests.

Hamburger Noodle Casserole

Irene Putman
Canal Fulton, OH

This quick & easy recipe uses basic ingredients,
comes together in a snap and tastes so good.

16-oz. pkg. wide egg noodles,
   uncooked
1-3/4 lbs. lean ground beef
1 onion, chopped
1 green pepper, chopped
1 t. salt

1 t. pepper
26-oz. can cream of
   mushroom soup
12-oz. pkg. shredded Cheddar
   cheese

Cook noodles according to package directions; drain. Meanwhile, in a
skillet over medium heat, brown beef with onion and green pepper.
Drain; season with salt and pepper. Combine cooked noodles, beef
mixture and soup; stir gently to mix. Transfer to a greased 13"x9" baking
pan; top with cheese. Bake, uncovered, at 325 degrees for 10 to
15 minutes, until bubbly and cheese is melted. Serves 6 to 8.

Spice up table decor in an instant. Arrange cinnamon sticks
around a pillar candle and attach with hot glue. Tie on a jute
bow and nestle in a shallow dish filled with whole cloves.

Food for Family & Friends

Spaghetti Pie

Wanda Baughman
Fayetteville, PA

This is a favorite with my family & friends...just add a tossed salad and garlic bread for a complete meal. These spaghetti pies can be made in advance and frozen for a quick family night supper too.

16-oz. pkg. spaghetti, uncooked
1/4 t. salt
3 eggs, divided
32-oz. jar favorite spaghetti
  sauce
16-oz. container ricotta cheese
2 T. Italian seasoning

1 t. garlic, chopped
16-oz. pkg. shredded
  mozzarella cheese
Optional: additional Italian
  seasoning
3/4 c. grated Parmesan cheese

Cook spaghetti according to package directions, adding salt to water. Drain; place in a large bowl and cool completely. Beat 2 eggs; add to spaghetti and mix thoroughly. Spray three, 9" pie plates with non-stick vegetable spray. Divide spaghetti mixture among pie plates, spreading along edges to create a crust. Spoon sauce into the center of each pie plate. Mix together ricotta cheese, remaining beaten egg, Italian seasoning and garlic; spread over sauce. Sprinkle with mozzarella cheese and additional Italian seasoning, if desired. Top pies with Parmesan cheese. Bake, uncovered, at 350 degrees for at least 30 minutes or until cheese is melted and bubbly. To serve, slice into wedges. Makes 3 pies, 6 servings each.

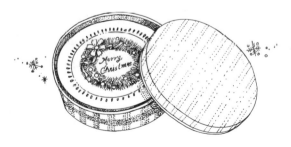

Go ahead and unpack the Christmas tableware early in December...even the simplest meal of Spaghetti Pie is special when served on holly-trimmed plates!

Western Hospitality Casserole

Cheryl Lagler
Zionsville, PA

Whenever I came home from college in the winter, my mom always made this tasty casserole. Since it makes two casseroles, you can serve one and freeze the other for later, or give it away...perfect to make for a new mom or someone who's recently home from the hospital.

3/4 c. all-purpose flour
2 t. salt
4 lbs. lean stew beef, sliced into
   1-inch cubes
1/3 c. oil, divided
2 cloves garlic, minced
6-oz. can tomato paste
3/4 c. dry red wine or beef broth

3-1/2 c. water
1 t. dried thyme
2 bay leaves
2 4-oz. cans mushroom pieces
8-oz. pkg. bowtie pasta, cooked
12-oz. pkg. shredded Cheddar
   cheese

Combine flour and salt in a shallow dish; coat beef with mixture. Heat half of oil in a large Dutch oven over medium-high heat; brown half of meat. Set aside cooked meat; brown remaining meat in remaining oil. Set aside meat. Add garlic to Dutch oven and sauté for one minute; add tomato paste, wine or broth, water, thyme, bay leaves and meat. Cover and simmer over low heat for 1-1/2 hours, or until meat is tender. Remove bay leaves; stir in mushrooms with liquid and cooked pasta. Divide mixture in half and pour into two lightly greased 13"x9" baking pans or two, 2-quart casserole dishes. Top with cheese and bake, uncovered, at 350 degrees for about 30 minutes. To freeze: prepare and fill casserole, but do not top with cheese. Let cool completely. Wrap securely with aluminum foil; place in freezer. When ready to serve, thaw at room temperature for 1-1/2 hours. Bake, covered, at 350 degrees for one hour. Uncover and top with cheese; bake 15 minutes longer to melt cheese. Makes 2 casseroles, 6 servings each.

Carrying in a casserole? Be sure to tie on a tag with the recipe! Clever tags can be made from holiday cards or colorful scrapbooking paper.

Food for Family & Friends

Cheesy Spinach & Sausage Bake

Rhonda Reeder
Ellicott City, MD

A hearty, filling casserole that everyone enjoys...a great make-ahead breakfast recipe too. Just prepare ahead and refrigerate overnight, then bake for 45 minutes in the morning.

1 lb. ground Italian sausage
8-oz. can tomato sauce
10-oz. pkg. frozen chopped
   spinach, thawed and drained

2 c. cottage cheese
1/2 c. grated Parmesan cheese
1 egg, beaten
2 c. shredded mozzarella cheese

Brown sausage in a large skillet over medium heat; stir in tomato sauce and heat through. Set aside. Combine spinach, cottage cheese, Parmesan cheese and egg in a large bowl. Mix well and spread into a lightly greased 13"x9" baking pan. Spoon sausage mixture over spinach mixture and top with mozzarella cheese. Bake at 350 degrees for 40 minutes. Serves 8.

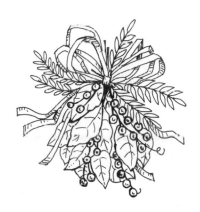

'Tis the season...hang a kissing ball in the doorway!
Make one by wrapping 2 embroidery hoops in
ribbon, then tie on a sprig of mistletoe.

Mac & Cheese Nuggets

Vickie
Gooseberry Patch

Little kids really go for these cheesy morsels...big kids too!

1/4 c. grated Parmesan cheese,
  divided
1-1/2 T. butter
2 T. all-purpose flour
3/4 c. milk
1-1/4 c. shredded Cheddar
  cheese

1/4 lb. American cheese slices,
  chopped
1 egg yolk, beaten
1/4 t. paprika
8-oz. pkg. elbow macaroni,
  cooked

Lightly grease mini muffin tins. Sprinkle with 2 tablespoons Parmesan cheese, tapping out excess. Melt butter in a large saucepan over medium heat. Stir in flour; cook for 2 minutes. Whisk in milk until boiling, about 5 minutes. Add Cheddar and American cheeses; remove from heat and stir until smooth. Whisk in egg yolk and paprika; fold in macaroni until well coated. Spoon rounded tablespoons of mixture into prepared tins; sprinkle with remaining Parmesan. Bake at 425 degrees until hot and golden, about 10 minutes. Cool for 5 minutes; carefully transfer to serving plate. Makes 4 dozen.

Set aside time for a little crafting with friends. Choose a favorite theme, like card and tag making, and everyone can bring along their favorite supplies to share.

Come for
Brunch

Creamy Chicken Bake

Angela Evans
Crystal Hill, VA

This is THE most requested recipe at our church. It took me years to get this right, but it is the best! I have a family of six with four hungry teenage boys, so this recipe usually is tripled. My mom likes asparagus instead of broccoli and my sister uses other flavors of soup...play with this recipe to suit any taste.

3 to 4 boneless, skinless
   chicken breasts
10-3/4 oz. can golden
   mushroom soup
10-3/4 oz. can cream of chicken
   and broccoli soup
8-oz. pkg. pasteurized process
   cheese spread, chopped

1/2 c. butter
10-oz. pkg. frozen chopped
   broccoli, cooked and drained
1 sleeve oval buttery crackers,
   crushed

In a large saucepan, cover chicken with water. Bring to a boil over medium heat; simmer for 25 to 30 minutes, until chicken is cooked through. Drain; let cool. Combine soups, cheese and butter in a separate saucepan. Cook and stir over medium-high heat, stirring often, until cheese is melted. Shred chicken; place in a buttered 13"x9" baking pan. Arrange broccoli over chicken; pour soup mixture over top. Sprinkle with crushed crackers. Bake, uncovered, at 350 degrees until golden and bubbly, about 30 minutes. Serves 6.

Celebrate the season with a holiday brunch buffet for friends & neighbors! It's a joyful time of year to renew old acquaintances while sharing scrumptious food together.

Come for *Brunch*

Savory Brunch Cups

Jo Ann
Gooseberry Patch

Little biscuit cups filled with Mom's pot pie filling...yummy!
They're perfectly portioned for brunch buffets too.

12-oz. tube refrigerated biscuit
    dough
1 T. butter
1 c. cooked turkey or chicken,
    cubed
1/2 c. frozen peas, thawed

4-oz. jar diced pimentos,
    drained
1/4 t. dried thyme
.87-oz. pkg. turkey or chicken
    gravy mix
1 c. milk

Press biscuits into bottom and up sides of 10 ungreased muffin cups.
Keep chilled until ready to fill. Melt butter in a skillet over medium
heat. Stir in turkey or chicken, peas, pimentos and thyme; heat
through. Blend gravy mix and milk; add to skillet. Cook, stirring
constantly, until gravy comes to a boil. Reduce heat and simmer,
stirring constantly, for one minute, or until thickened. Spoon
hot mixture into prepared biscuit cups. Bake at 375 degrees for
15 minutes. Makes 10 servings.

Just for fun, set out snowman-shaped candy
marshmallows for folks to float in their hot cocoa!

Pecan Flapjacks

Kelly Hall
Butler, MO

These tender pancakes have been a part of my family's traditional Christmas breakfast ever since my cousin in Estes Park, Colorado gave me this recipe years ago.

1-1/2 c. whole-wheat flour
1 c. all-purpose flour
1 c. long-cooking oats,
    uncooked
1/2 c. yellow cornmeal
1 T. baking powder
2 t. baking soda

1 t. salt
3/4 c. chilled butter, diced
4 eggs, beaten
4 c. buttermilk
1/2 c. honey
1 c. chopped pecans

Process flours, oats, cornmeal, baking powder, baking soda and salt together in a food processor until well blended. Add butter; process until mixture resembles coarse meal and set aside. Whisk eggs and buttermilk together in a large bowl; whisk in honey. Stir in flour mixture; fold in nuts. Drop by 1/4 cupfuls onto a preheated, well greased griddle; cook until golden on both sides. Serves 8 to 10.

For extra-special pancakes or French toast, whip up some maple butter in no time. Just blend 1/2 cup butter with 3/4 cup maple syrup.

Come for *Brunch*

Fantastic Stuffed French Toast

Paige Miller
Mansfield, OH

I love French toast, and this recipe is out of this world!

5 eggs, beaten
2/3 c. heavy cream
2 t. cinnamon
2 8-oz. pkgs. cream cheese,
   softened
1 t. vanilla extract

2 loaves Vienna bread, sliced
   into 3-inch thick slices
12-oz. jar apricot preserves
1/2 c. orange, banana &
   strawberry juice blend

Whisk together eggs, cream and cinnamon; set aside. Beat cream cheese and vanilla with an electric mixer. Set aside. Slice 3/4 of the way into one edge of each bread slice, creating a pocket. Spoon some of the cream cheese mixture into each bread pocket. Dip slices into egg mixture on both sides. On a griddle over medium heat sprayed with non-stick vegetable spray, fry until golden on both sides. Meanwhile, mix preserves and juice in a small saucepan; simmer over medium heat until combined. Spoon warm preserves mixture over slices of French toast. Serves 6.

It's easy to mix & match...set a festive table with items you already have! Green transferware serving bowls, sparkling white porcelain dinner plates and ruby-red stemmed glasses combine beautifully with Christmas dinnerware and with each other.

Crustless Ham & Swiss Pie

Susan Paffenroth
Johnson City, TN

This pie couldn't be easier to stir up...it even makes its own crust.

2 c. cooked ham, shredded
  or diced
1 c. shredded Swiss cheese
1/3 c. onion, chopped
4 eggs, beaten

2 c. milk
1 c. biscuit baking mix
pepper, paprika and dried
  parsley to taste

Layer ham, cheese and onion in the bottom of a greased
10" deep-dish pie plate; set aside. Combine eggs, milk and baking
mix in a blender; process for 15 seconds. Pour over ingredients in
pie plate. Sprinkle with pepper, paprika and parsley to taste. Bake
at 400 degrees for 30 to 40 minutes, or until golden and a knife
tip comes out clean when inserted in center. Let stand for about
10 minutes to set; cut into wedges. Serves 6.

For buffets or dinner parties, save time by rolling up flatware
in colorful napkins, tying with ribbon bows and stacking
in a flat basket. Even kids can help with this well in
advance of the party...one less last-minute task!

Come for *Brunch*

Christmas Market Potatoes

Penny Bryant
Surprise, AZ

When we were stationed in Germany with the Air Force, my husband Ken, our daughter Victoria and I went to the many Christmas markets that every town held during November and December. At every one, this dish was being made right on the street...it was always warm and comforting. Now that we are back in the States, I enjoy making it often.

2 T. olive oil
16-oz. pkg. thick-cut bacon,
   sliced into 1/2-inch pieces
1 to 2 yellow onions, chopped

1 to 2 cloves garlic, chopped
5 lbs. russet potatoes, cubed
   and cooked
salt and pepper to taste

Heat oil over medium heat in a very large skillet with a lid. Add bacon and cook until almost crisp. Add onions; continue cooking until bacon is done and onions are soft and almost translucent. Add garlic; cook for one to 2 minutes. Add potatoes; cook for 2 to 3 minutes. Using a broad spatula or pancake turner, flatten mixture in skillet. Cook without stirring for 3 minutes; add salt and pepper to taste. Begin turning the mixture over in large sections. Cook on other side until golden. Sprinkle with salt and pepper again as needed. Makes 6 to 8 servings.

Put a slow cooker to work on the buffet...set on low,
it can keep sausage gravy, scrambled eggs or other
breakfast foods piping-hot and delicious.

Emma's Gingerbread Muffins

Bernadette Dobias
Houston, TX

*I received this recipe from a friend's mother who has since passed away.
They were a real hit when she served the muffins at a luncheon for her
bridge club. The muffins are very moist and spicy...I bake them in mini
muffin tins to keep from eating too many!*

1 c. sugar	3 c. all-purpose flour
1/2 c. butter, softened	2 t. cinnamon
1/2 c. shortening	2 t. ground ginger
3 eggs	1 t. nutmeg
1/2 c. molasses	1-3/4 t. baking soda
1/2 c. golden or light corn syrup	1 c. buttermilk

Blend together sugar, butter and shortening. Add eggs, one at a time,
beating after each addition. Add molasses and corn syrup; beat just
until blended. Set aside. Sift together flour and spices. Dissolve baking
soda in buttermilk. Add milk mixture to butter mixture alternately with
flour mixture, stirring just until combined. Fill greased and floured
muffin tins 2/3 full. Bake at 350 degrees for about 15 minutes, or
until a toothpick inserted in center comes out clean. Makes 2 dozen.

A tiered cake stand looks inviting on a buffet and saves space
too. Fill alternate levels with bite-size goodies and Christmas
greenery, tucking in some shiny ornaments for holiday sparkle.

Come for *Brunch*

Monkey Muffins

Alicia Meharg
Gatesville, TX

I created this recipe for my little "monkeys," my three kids, when I had some really ripe bananas but not all the ingredients needed for our usual banana bread. Now my kids get so excited when they notice the bananas are turning brown...that means it's time for Monkey Muffins!

1/2 c. butter, softened
1 c. sugar
1 egg, beaten
1 t. vanilla extract
1-1/2 c. ripe banana, mashed
1-1/2 c. all-purpose flour

1 t. baking powder
1 t. baking soda
1/2 t. salt
1 c. mini semi-sweet chocolate
  chips
1/2 c. chopped pecans

Blend butter and sugar. Add egg and vanilla; beat until thoroughly combined. Blend in banana. Combine flour, baking powder, baking soda and salt; add to butter mixture and mix well. Stir in chocolate chips and pecans. Fill greased mini muffins pans 1/2 full. Bake at 350 degrees for 12 to 14 minutes. Cool in pan 5 minutes; remove to a wire rack to cool completely. Makes 4 dozen.

At Christmas, when old friends are meeting
We give that long-loved joyous greeting...
"Merry Christmas!"
– Dorothy Brown Thompson

Caramel Breakfast Wreath

JoAnne Murdock
Hilliard, OH

*This make-ahead recipe is wonderful for morning gatherings
with family & friends! My family really enjoys this recipe.*

1 c. chopped pecans, divided
16 frozen white dinner rolls
3-1/2 oz. pkg. cook & serve
   butterscotch pudding mix

3/4 c. brown sugar, packed
1/2 c. butter, melted

The night before, sprinkle half the pecans in the bottom of a Bundt®
pan that has been sprayed with non-stick vegetable spray. Arrange
dinner rolls on top of pecans; sprinkle with pudding mix. Mix brown
sugar and butter together; pour over rolls. Spread remaining pecans
over top. Place pan in a cold oven and let stand overnight to rise. In
the morning, remove pan from the oven and preheat to 325 degrees.
Return pan to oven; bake for 30 minutes. Turn pan upside-down onto
a platter and serve. Serves 8 to 12.

Charming, yet oh-so-simple...slip a posy-filled mini
bud vase into the center of a festive Bundt® cake.

Come for *Brunch*

Orange Blossom Rolls

Kathy Grashoff
Fort Wayne, IN

Mmm...can't you just smell these baking?

1 loaf frozen bread dough,
   thawed
1/4 c. butter, softened
2 T. sugar

2 T. plus 1 t. orange zest
2 c. powdered sugar
3 T. orange juice

On a lightly floured surface, roll thawed dough into a 14-inch by 9-inch rectangle. Combine butter, sugar and 2 tablespoons zest; spread over dough, leaving a 1/2-inch border around edges. Roll dough up, jelly-roll style, starting at one long side; pinch long seam to seal (do not seal ends). Cut roll into 3/4-inch slices; place slices in a greased 13"x9" baking pan. Cover and let rise in a warm place, about 85 degrees, for 40 minutes, or until double in bulk. Bake at 400 degrees for 20 to 25 minutes, or until golden. Whisk together powdered sugar, juice and remaining zest until smooth; drizzle over hot rolls. Makes 1-1/2 dozen.

Don't put away those Christmas cookie cutters just yet! Use them to shape pancakes or cut shapes from the centers of French toast...even make the cutest pats of butter.

Festive Turkey Enchiladas

Michelle Sheridan
Delaware, OH

Zesty enchiladas filled with seasonal flavors.

2 to 2-1/2 c. cooked turkey, shredded
15-oz. can black beans, drained and rinsed
16-oz. can whole-berry cranberry sauce, divided
1-1/2 c. salsa, divided
1 c. shredded Colby-Jack cheese, divided

1/2 c. sour cream
3 green onions, sliced
1/4 c. fresh cilantro, snipped
1 t. ground cumin
1/2 t. salt
1/2 t. pepper
8 8-inch flour tortillas
1 t. hot pepper sauce
Optional: green onions, sliced

In a large bowl, stir together turkey, beans, one cup cranberry sauce, 1/2 cup salsa, 3/4 cup cheese, sour cream, green onions and seasonings. Spoon 2/3 cup filling onto each tortilla; roll up tortillas. Place seam-side down in a lightly greased 3-quart casserole dish; set aside. Stir together remaining cranberry sauce and salsa; add hot sauce and spoon over tortillas. Cover with aluminum foil; bake at 350 degrees for 45 minutes. Uncover; top with remaining cheese and bake an additional 5 to 10 minutes, until heated through and cheese is melted. Garnish with additional green onions, if desired. Makes 8 servings.

Write guests' names on shiny round ornaments with a gold glitter paint pen and heap them in a tall glass trifle bowl. They'll double as tabletop decoration and as take-home gifts for guests.

Cheesy Chicken Pockets

Liz Gist
London, England

This started out as a recipe for a cheeseburger casserole made with crescent rolls. I just kept changing out ingredients until I'd created these tasty chicken pockets...everyone loves them!

2 T. butter
2 T. all-purpose flour
1/3 c. milk
1/2 c. chicken broth
1/2 t. nutmeg
1/4 t. salt
1/4 t. pepper
1-1/2 c. shredded Cheddar
   cheese

3 slices bacon, crisply cooked
   and crumbled
2 boneless, skinless chicken
   breasts, cooked and chopped
2 sheets frozen puff pastry,
   thawed and quartered

In a medium saucepan, melt butter over medium-high heat. Stir in flour and mix well. Add milk, broth and seasonings; mix well. Bring to a boil over medium heat; cook until thick enough to coat the back of a spoon. Stir in cheese and bacon; mix until cheese melts. Stir in chicken, making sure each piece is coated with sauce. Arrange 4 quartered pieces of puff pastry one inch apart on a greased baking sheet. Spoon 1/4 of chicken mixture onto each piece. Top with remaining puff pastry; press edges down with a fork to seal. Bake at 400 degrees for 15 to 18 minutes. Let cool for 5 minutes before serving. Makes 4 servings.

Remember to place larger, more showy floral arrangements like poinsettias on a buffet table and smaller ones on the dining table, so guests can talk and visit.

Hot Cinnamon Twisters

Pat Habiger
Spearville, KS

Easy and fun to make with grandkids. The best memories are from the kitchen, sharing food and laughs.

12-oz. tube refrigerated
  buttermilk biscuits
1/3 c. sugar

1-1/4 t. cinnamon
1/3 c. margarine, melted

Slightly flatten each biscuit and cut a slit through the center. Mix sugar and cinnamon; set aside. Dip each biscuit in melted margarine, then in sugar mixture. Pull, then twist each biscuit. Place on a greased baking sheet; bake at 425 degrees for about 10 minutes, until golden. Serve warm. Makes 10.

Show off Christmas snapshots from years past in a wire card holder. Choose a common theme like a visit to Santa, pets in holiday costumes or kids around the Christmas tree. Whether photos are sweet or silly, family & friends will love taking a trip down memory lane with you.

Come for *Brunch*

Chocolate Eggnog

Valarie Dennard
Palatka, FL

A great no-fuss recipe for jazzing up store-bought eggnog.

2 qts. eggnog
16-oz. can chocolate syrup
Optional: 1/2 c. light rum

1 c. whipping cream
2 T. powdered sugar
Garnish: baking cocoa

Combine eggnog, chocolate syrup and rum, if using, in a punch bowl, stirring well. Beat whipping cream with an electric mixer on high speed until foamy. Add powdered sugar; continue beating until stiff peaks form. Dollop whipped cream over eggnog, sift cocoa over top. Serve immediately. Makes 3 quarts.

Holiday Wassail

Lori Downing
Bradenton, FL

We have had this recipe in our family for years. My mom would make it and put it on the woodburning stove for us to serve ourselves. You could smell it throughout the whole house.

64-oz. can apple juice
64-oz. can pineapple juice
1/3 c. lemon juice

1/4 c. honey
1/4 t. nutmeg
4-inch cinnamon stick

Combine all ingredients in a large stockpot over medium-low heat; simmer until hot. Makes one gallon.

Company Breakfast Casserole

Jena Buckler
Bloomington Springs, TN

*For a southwest flair, replace the mushrooms with a small can
of sliced olives, add Monterey Jack cheese instead of
Cheddar and serve with spicy salsa on the side.*

16-oz. pkg. shredded frozen
  hashbrowns, thawed
1 onion, chopped and divided
1 lb. ground pork sausage,
  browned and drained
1 green pepper, chopped
4-oz. can sliced mushrooms,
  drained

1/2 to 1 c. shredded Cheddar
  cheese
1 doz. eggs, beaten
1-1/2 c. milk
salt and pepper to taste
Optional: garlic salt to taste

Spread hashbrowns in a lightly greased 9"x9" baking pan. Layer
ingredients as follows: half the onion, sausage, remaining onion,
green pepper, mushrooms and cheese. In a separate bowl, mix eggs,
milk and seasonings very well. Pour egg mixture over top of
casserole; cover with aluminum foil and refrigerate overnight. In
the morning, bake, covered, at 350 degrees for 45 to 60 minutes.
Uncover and bake an additional 15 minutes, or until a knife inserted
in center comes out clean. Serves 8 to 10.

Hand-written menus lend a personal
touch to any table. Cut colored paper to
fit a picture frame and write on details...
be sure to call out much-anticipated
dishes like Aunt June's Yummy
Potatoes and Grandma's Sweet Rolls!
Decorate with holiday stickers or
clippings from Christmas cards.

Come for *Brunch*

Kiddies' Favorite Quiche

Stephanie Onick
El Paso, TX

My kids BEG for this potato-crusted quiche...they want it for breakfast, lunch, snacks and dinnertime! Sometimes I make one on Sunday evening to have for school lunches and after-school snacks. They never tire of it. My husband loves it, too.

3 c. frozen shredded
   hashbrowns, thawed
3 T. butter, melted
1 c. cooked ham or bacon, diced
1 c. shredded Cheddar cheese

3 eggs, beaten
1/2 c. milk
1/2 t. salt
1/4 t. pepper

Press hashbrowns between paper towels to remove any excess moisture. Pat hashbrowns into a lightly greased 8" pie plate to form a crust; drizzle with butter. Bake at 425 degrees for 25 minutes. Remove from oven; turn down oven temperature to 350 degrees. Combine ham or bacon and cheese; mix well and spoon into baked crust. Whisk eggs, milk, salt and pepper in a large bowl. Pour over ham and cheese. Bake at 350 degrees until quiche sets, 25 to 30 minutes. Slice into wedges. Serves 8.

Breakfast with Santa...what fun! Ask a family friend to play Santa for the children at your holiday brunch. They'll love sharing secrets with the jolly old elf over waffles and hot cocoa. At the party's end, have Santa hand out little bags of "Reindeer Food" (cereal mixed with colored jimmies) for kids to sprinkle on the lawn on Christmas Eve.

Kathleen's Mountain Waffles

Kathleen Walker
Mountain Center, CA

Watching my great-grandmother bake from scratch inspired me to learn how to do the same. Now my children ask me to make these waffles for them when they come to visit my husband and me.

3 eggs, separated
2 t. baking powder
2-1/2 t. powdered sugar
1/4 t. salt

2 c. whipping cream
1-1/2 c. all-purpose flour
1 T. butter, melted
Garnish: maple syrup

With an electric mixer on high setting, beat egg whites until stiff peaks form; set aside. In a separate bowl, beat egg yolks. Add baking powder, powdered sugar and salt to yolks and beat again until fully blended. Add cream and beat again for several minutes, mixing in flour and butter. Fold in egg whites. Pour about 1/2 cup batter into a preheated waffle iron that has been sprayed with non-stick vegetable spray. Bake as manufacturer directs. Serve with warm maple syrup. Makes 6 to 8 servings.

When guests are coming for brunch, a little kitchen prep the night before is really helpful. Whisk up eggs for scrambling, stir together dry ingredients for waffles and lay out tableware ahead of time...in the morning, just tie on your prettiest apron and you'll be a relaxed hostess!

Come for *Brunch*

Sweet Potato Waffles

Mary Ann Dell
Phoenixville, PA

Serve topped with dollops of whipped cream and a sprinkle of chopped pecans for an extra-special treat.

1 c. sweet potatoes, peeled,
   cooked and mashed
1-1/4 c. buttermilk
1 egg, beaten
1 T. oil

2 c. biscuit baking mix
1/4 c. sugar
1/2 t. cinnamon
Garnish: powdered sugar

In a large bowl, combine mashed sweet potatoes, buttermilk, egg and oil. In a separate bowl, whisk together baking mix, sugar and cinnamon. Stir sweet potato mixture into dry ingredients to make a fairly thick batter. Spoon 1/2 to 3/4 cup batter into a preheated waffle iron that has been sprayed with non stick vegetable spray. Bake as manufacturer directs. Sprinkle with powdered sugar. Serves 6.

Create a charming tea tray. Have a favorite vintage Christmas card enlarged on a color copier. Place it in a decorative old frame. Surround the image with bits of vintage lace or rick rack...so clever!

Confetti Cheesecake

Suzanne Varnes
Palatka, FL

This is a recipe I have made many times...my guests always enjoy it!
Serve it like a cheese ball with an assortment of crisp crackers, or
slice thinly and serve with a crisp green salad for a light lunch.

1-1/2 c. round buttery crackers,
  crushed
1/2 c. butter, melted
2 8-oz. pkgs. cream cheese,
  softened
2 eggs
1/3 c. all-purpose flour
8-oz. container sour cream

1-1/2 c. green pepper, finely
  chopped
3/4 c. carrot, peeled and
  shredded
1/4 c. onion, finely chopped
1/4 t. salt
1/4 t. white pepper

Combine cracker crumbs and butter; press into bottom of an
ungreased 9" or 10" springform pan. Bake at 300 degrees for
10 minutes; remove from oven. In a large bowl, beat cream cheese
until fluffy; add eggs, one at a time. Stir in flour, mixing well. Add
remaining ingredients, folding to combine vegetables well into batter.
Pour into baked crust and bake at 300 degrees for one hour. Turn
oven off; let cheesecake cool in oven for another hour before
refrigerating. At serving time, remove outer ring of springform pan.
Serves 10 to 12.

Live music makes any gathering extra special for guests.
Ask a nearby school to recommend a music student who
would enjoy playing Christmas carols on piano or violin.

Come for *Brunch*

Spinach & Bacon Mini Quiches

Kendall Hale
Lynn, MA

Tempting little bite-size tarts!

2 9-inch pie crusts
2 eggs, beaten
1/2 c. sour cream
3/4 t. mustard
1/4 t. salt
1/8 t. nutmeg
1/4 t. cayenne pepper

3/4 c. shredded Swiss cheese
3 T. onion, chopped
2 T. frozen chopped spinach,
     drained and pressed dry
3 slices bacon, crisply cooked
     and crumbled
Garnish: nutmeg

Place pie crusts on a lightly floured surface. Using a 2-3/4" round biscuit cutter, cut 30 circles out of crusts. Gently fit circles into bottom and up sides of ungreased mini muffin cups, pressing edges against rims. Set aside. Whisk together eggs, sour cream, mustard and seasonings; stir in cheese, onion, spinach and bacon. Spoon one tablespoon filling into each muffin cup; sprinkle with extra nutmeg. Bake at 400 degrees for 15 to 20 minutes, until golden. Serve hot. Makes 2-1/2 dozen.

Dress up plain orange juice in a jiffy! Add a splash of fizzy ginger ale and serve it up in stemmed glasses trimmed with ribbon bows...an oh-so-simple touch that guests will remember.

Sour Cream Streusel Coffee Cake

Kathy Terry
Delaware, OH

This sweet, nutty coffee cake can be made a day ahead...what a timesaver for busy hostesses! Cool completely, then wrap in aluminum foil and store at room temperature.

1-1/4 c. walnuts, coarsely chopped
1-1/4 c. brown sugar, packed
4-1/2 t. cinnamon
4-1/2 t. baking cocoa
3 c. cake flour
1-1/2 t. baking powder
1-1/2 t. baking soda
3/4 t. salt
3/4 c. butter, softened
1-1/2 c. sugar
3 eggs
1 T. vanilla extract
16-oz. container sour cream
1 c. powdered sugar
1 T. milk

Mix walnuts, brown sugar, cinnamon and cocoa in a small bowl; set aside. Sift flour, baking powder, baking soda and salt into a medium bowl; set aside. With an electric mixer on medium speed, beat butter and sugar in large bowl. Beat in eggs, one at a time; mix in vanilla. Add flour mixture and sour cream alternately into butter mixture in 3 additions; beat on high speed for one minute. Pour 1/3 of batter into a buttered 12-cup Bundt® pan; sprinkle with half of nut mixture. Add another 1/3 of batter; sprinkle with remaining nut mixture. Spoon remaining batter over top. Bake at 350 degrees until a toothpick inserted near center comes out clean, about one hour. Cool cake in pan on a wire rack for 10 minutes; run a knife around pan sides to loosen. Turn cake out onto rack and cool for one hour. Transfer to a serving platter. Whisk powdered sugar and milk together in a small bowl and drizzle over cake. May be served warm or at room temperature. Makes 8 to 10 servings.

A fringed red plaid throw makes a festive runner for a brunch table.

Come for *Brunch*

Eskimo Doughnuts

Frances Pikok
Barrow, AK

Everyone here in Barrow, Alaska loves these homemade doughnuts.

2 envs. active dry yeast
2-1/2 c. warm water
1-1/2 to 2 T. sugar
6 to 8 c. all-purpose flour

1 T. salt
6 to 8 c. shortening for deep
   frying

Mix yeast into very warm water, about 110 to 115 degrees. Stir in sugar and set aside. Mix together flour and salt in a large bowl. Slowly add in yeast mixture to flour mixture. Combine well until dough forms; knead on a floured surface for several minutes. Do not overwork dough. Place in a greased bowl, turning once to coat. Cover and let rise in a warm place for 1-1/2 hours, or until double in bulk. Punch down dough; shape by hand into rings or twists. Heat shortening to 350 degrees in a deep saucepan. Add doughnuts, a few at a time; fry until golden on all sides. Drain on paper towels. Makes 2 to 3 dozen.

Offer guests fun toppers for their coffees...flavored creamers,
mini chocolate chips and fluffy whipped topping. Yum!

Eggs Goldenrod

LuAnn Currier
Mount Vernon, OH

When I was little, my mom used to make this dish for me. It was one of my favorite meals. I remember coming home for lunch in grade school, and Mom would have this ready for me. After lunch, I would sit in the rocking chair with her until it was time to go back to school...such good memories!

3 T. butter
3 T. all-purpose flour
1 c. milk, warmed
salt and paprika to taste

6 eggs, hard-boiled, peeled
  and halved
6 slices bread, toasted and
  generously buttered

Melt butter in a small, heavy saucepan over low heat; blend in flour. Cook and stir over low heat for 4 to 5 minutes. Slowly add milk, stirring constantly. Continue cooking slowly until thick and smooth. Add salt and paprika to taste; dice egg whites and stir them into the sauce. To serve, place toast on 6 luncheon plates; spoon sauce over toast. Press egg yolks through a sieve or grate over sauce. Serve at once. Serves 6.

Vintage salt & pepper shakers, in the shape of snowmen
or Mr. & Mrs. Santa, add a touch of holiday cheer
to any table and a smile to guests' faces.

Come for *Brunch*

Zesty Brunch Quiche

Patty Schroyer
Baxter, IA

Try using peach or apricot salsa for a whole new taste.

1 c. shredded Cheddar cheese
4 slices bacon, crisply cooked
    and crumbled
2 green onions, thinly sliced

9-inch frozen pie crust
3 eggs, beaten
1/2 c. milk
1/2 c. salsa

Sprinkle cheese, bacon and onions into pie crust; set aside. Whisk eggs, milk and salsa together; pour into pie crust. Carefully place on a baking sheet; bake at 375 degrees for 35 minutes. Let stand 10 minutes before slicing. Makes 6 servings.

Tina's Creamy Bacon Crescents

Tina Goodpusture
Meadowview, VA

These crescent rolls are sooo good! At church functions,
I get many compliments on them...you will too.

8-oz. tube refrigerated
    crescent rolls
8-oz. container whipped
    cream cheese

8 slices bacon

Separate rolls. Spread with cream cheese and roll up as indicated on package directions. Wrap one slice bacon around each roll; place on an ungreased baking sheet. Bake at 350 degrees for 15 to 20 minutes, until golden. Serve warm or cooled. Makes 6 to 8 servings.

Scrambled Eggs in Toast Cups

Stacie Avner
Delaware, OH

Crisp little toast cups filled with creamy eggs...
so appealing on a brunch buffet!

10 extra-thin slices bread,
　crusts trimmed
2 T. butter, softened and divided
4 eggs, beaten
1/4 c. milk
1/8 t. salt

1/8 t. pepper
1 c. cooked ham, diced
3/4 c. shredded Cheddar cheese,
　divided
1/3 c. canned mushrooms,
　chopped

Spread bread slices with one tablespoon butter; press into a buttered muffin tin to form cups. Bake at 375 degrees for 3 minutes; remove from oven. Whisk together eggs, milk, salt and pepper. Add ham, 1/4 cup cheese and mushrooms; mix well. Melt remaining butter in a skillet over medium-low heat. Pour in egg mixture; cook and stir until eggs are barely set. Spoon into toast cups. Bake at 375 degrees for 10 to 15 minutes, until golden. Sprinkle with remaining cheese; return to oven until cheese melts, about 2 minutes. Makes 10 servings.

Turn refrigerated cinnamon rolls into snowmen. Arrange rolls in a snowman shape on a baking sheet and bake as directed. Top with fluffy white icing and add faces with bits of dried fruit or mini candies. Festive...and fun!

Chilly-Day Soups

Snowy Day Chili

Kathie Poritz
Burlington, WI

Here in Wisconsin snow is inevitable, but shoveling sidewalks isn't so dreaded when there's a pot of chili simmering on the stove!

2 lbs. ground beef or venison
2 c. chopped onion
15-oz. can kidney beans,
    drained and rinsed
4 c. canned or homemade
    tomato sauce
4 c. water
6-oz. can tomato paste
1/4 c. Worcestershire sauce
2 T. brown sugar, packed

1 T. seasoned salt
1 T. lemon juice
3 bay leaves
chili powder to taste
Optional: hot pepper sauce
    to taste
Garnish: shredded Cheddar
    cheese, chopped onion,
    sour cream, corn chips

In a large stockpot over medium heat, brown meat; drain. Stir in remaining ingredients except garnish. Reduce heat; simmer for 3 to 4 hours, stirring occasionally. Discard bay leaves; serve with desired toppings. Makes 8 to 10 servings.

Invite neighbors over for a Chili Dump...a fun tradition in the
Midwest. Each guest brings a batch of her own red chili,
and they're all poured into one big kettle together.
You just provide the buttery cornbread.

Canadian Potato & Cheese Soup

Caressa Nusz
Wichita, KS

My best friend gave me this recipe long ago. She is a wonderful cook and friend. I make this soup all winter long for my entire family...it's even tastier as leftovers!

6 potatoes, peeled and cubed
3 stalks celery, chopped
2 carrots, peeled and chopped
1/2 onion, chopped
3 to 4 cubes chicken bouillon

dried parsley to taste
1/4 to 1/2 lb. pasteurized
   process cheese spread, cubed
5-oz. can evaporated milk
salt and pepper to taste

In a large stockpot, combine vegetables, bouillon cubes and parsley. Add water to cover vegetables. Cook over medium-high heat until potatoes are tender, about 20 to 25 minutes. Stir in cheese, evaporated milk, salt and pepper. Cook until cheese is melted, about 5 to 10 minutes. Using a potato masher, mash potatoes enough to thicken soup. Makes 6 to 8 servings.

Tote along a vintage thermos filled with hot soup on a visit to the Christmas tree farm...it'll really hit the spot! Before ladling in the soup, prewarm the thermos with hot water for 10 minutes.

Mom's Corn Chowder

Jane Hrabak
Belle Plaine, IA

My boys always hoped this thick, rich soup would be awaiting them when we'd drive to see Grandma & Grandpa on a cold winter's night. They would pile on the cheese and dig right in! My mom always beamed at their great appetites, but I knew it was her great cooking.

2 c. potatoes, peeled and diced
1 c. celery, diced
1/2 c. onion, diced
2 c. water
1 bay leaf
1/2 t. dried marjoram
5 to 6 slices bacon
2 to 3 T. all-purpose flour

2 14-3/4 oz. cans creamed corn
2 to 3 c. frozen corn
14-1/2 oz. can diced tomatoes
1-1/4 c. milk
1/8 t. dried parsley
Garnish: shredded Cheddar
  cheese

Place first 6 ingredients in a soup pot or Dutch oven over medium heat. Simmer, uncovered, until potatoes are almost tender, about 20 to 25 minutes. In a separate large soup pot, cook bacon over medium-high heat until crisp; remove bacon from soup pot. Stir flour into bacon drippings until blended. Add potato mixture and remaining ingredients except cheese. Cover and continue to simmer for about one hour. At serving time, discard bay leaf; garnish portions with shredded cheese as desired. Serves 8 to 10.

Fill a big Mason jar with wrapped candies and place it in the center of the dining table...don't forget to count them first! Ask everyone to guess how many candies are in the jar... send it home with the person whose guess is the closest!

Chilly-Day *Soups*

Bethany Wild Rice Soup

Susan Owens
Redlands, CA

Our church family always gathers in early December for a "Hanging of the Greens" night. It starts off with Christmas carols and a soup supper...my favorite is this wild rice soup.

2 c. wild rice, uncooked
2 T. butter
2 sweet onions, chopped
1/2 c. all-purpose flour
2 qts. chicken broth
4 carrots, peeled and shredded
6 c. cooked chicken breast, shredded

1/2 c. milk
2/3 c. blanched slivered almonds
1/4 c. fresh parsley, chopped
1/2 t. salt
1/2 t. pepper

Cover rice with water in a medium saucepan. Simmer over medium-low heat for 30 minutes. Drain; rinse rice and set aside. In a large soup pot, melt butter over medium heat. Add onions and cook until translucent. Stir in flour; mix well. Stir in broth, a little at a time; cook until slightly thickened. Add remaining ingredients and cooked rice. Reduce heat; simmer for 25 minutes. Makes 10 to 12 servings.

I wish we could put up some of the Christmas spirit
in jars and open a jar of it every month.
– Harlan Miller

Tomato-Ravioli Soup

Heather Quinn
Gilmer, TX

This soup has a light, smooth flavor...there's always an empty pot!

1 lb. ground beef
28-oz. can crushed tomatoes
6-oz. can tomato paste
2 c. water
1-1/2 c. onion, chopped
2 cloves garlic, minced
1/4 c. fresh parsley, chopped
3/4 t. dried basil
1/2 t. dried oregano
1/4 t. dried thyme
1/2 t. onion salt
1/2 t. salt
1/4 t. pepper
1/2 t. sugar
9-oz. pkg. frozen cheese ravioli
1/4 c. grated Parmesan cheese

In a Dutch oven, cook beef over medium heat until no longer pink; drain. Stir in tomatoes, tomato paste, water, onion, garlic and seasonings. Bring to a boil. Reduce heat; cover and simmer for 30 minutes. Cook ravioli as package directs; drain. Add ravioli to soup and heat through. Stir in Parmesan cheese; serve immediately. Makes 6 to 8 servings.

Show off Christmas cards...attach them to a length of rick rack and hang on either side of a doorway.

Herbed Garlic Bread

Cherylann Smith
Efland, NC

*A must-have with lasagna! Leftover slices make tasty
salad croutons...just cube and re-toast or fry them.*

1/2 c. butter, softened
1 sprig fresh rosemary
2 cloves garlic, pressed
1 t. Italian seasoning
1 t. dried basil
1 t. dried oregano

1 t. dried thyme
1 t. dried savory
1 t. dried marjoram
1 loaf country-style bread, sliced
    1-inch thick

Combine butter and seasonings in a large microwave-safe mug.
Microwave on high setting for one minute, until butter is melted; stir.
Brush over both sides of bread slices; place bread on an ungreased
baking sheet. Bake at 350 degrees until toasted, about 15 minutes.
Makes about 12 servings.

Bake up an extra loaf of bread to share, wrapped in
a tea towel...such a neighborly gesture!

Pepper Jack-Crab Bisque

Wendy Ball
Battle Creek, MI

My husband and I had enjoyed a soup like this when dining out with our good friends, Rick and Carolyn. My efforts to recreate it really paid off...they love it, and it's my husband's favorite too!

2 T. butter
2 stalks celery, finely chopped
1 onion, finely chopped
2 10-3/4 oz. cans tomato
   bisque or tomato soup
2-1/2 c. whipping cream or
   half-and-half

3 8-oz. pkgs. imitation
   crabmeat, flaked
1-1/2 c. shredded Pepper-Jack
   cheese

Melt butter in a stockpot over medium heat. Add celery and onion; cook until softened. Add soup, cream or half-and-half and crabmeat. Simmer over low heat until heated through; stir in cheese. If too thick, add a little more cream or half-and-half as desired. Makes 4 to 6 servings.

Make fragrant fire starters from ingredients around the kitchen. Mix together one-inch cinnamon sticks, dried orange peel and whole cloves. Tuck inside a cardboard tube and wrap the roll with kraft paper, securing the ends with ribbon. Toss several in a gift tote for gift-giving.

Chilly-Day *Soups*

Shrimp Chowder

Mary Beaney
Bourbonnais, IL

Serve with a loaf of hot sourdough bread and a big crock
of creamery butter...pure comfort food!

5 onions, chopped
1/2 c. butter
4 potatoes, peeled and diced
3 c. boiling water
salt and pepper to taste
3 c. milk

16-oz. pkg. pasteurized process
   cheese spread, cubed
1-1/2 lbs. small shrimp, cooked
   and peeled
Optional: fresh parsley, minced

In a soup pot over medium heat, sauté onions in butter until tender.
Add potatoes and boiling water; reduce heat and simmer until potatoes
are tender. Stir in salt and pepper to taste; set aside. Combine milk
and cheese in a large sauccpan. Cook over medium heat until cheese
melts; stir into chowder. Add shrimp; simmer over medium-low heat
for 20 minutes. Garnish portions with parsley, if desired. Serves
4 to 6.

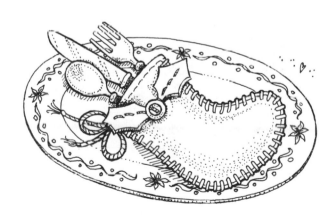

Tuck flatware into a mini Christmas stocking
to set at each place setting...how festive!

Roast Chicken-Corn Tortilla Soup

Sherry Noble
Kennett, MO

Garnish with quick-fried strips of red corn tortillas.

1 deli roasted chicken, cut into
   bite-size pieces
4 c. chicken broth
1/2 c. chipotle salsa
1/2 c. tequila lime salsa
1 to 2 c. corn tortilla chips,
   crushed

juice of 1/2 lime
1/2 c. fresh cilantro, chopped
salt and pepper
Optional: shredded Cheddar
   cheese, sour cream

Combine chicken, broth and salsas in a large saucepan over medium-high heat. Add tortilla chips and simmer for 10 minutes. Stir in lime juice, cilantro, salt and pepper. Serve immediately, garnished with cheese and sour cream, if desired. Serves 4.

Send home a container of hearty homemade soup with
a college student or an older person who lives alone...
a gesture that will be much appreciated.

Chilly-Day *Soups*

Southwestern Stew

Claudia Waggoner
North Port, FL

*One of my husband's favorite meals....friends always
ask me for the recipe.*

1 to 2 lbs. boneless pork chops,
  cubed
16-oz. can pinto beans, drained
  and rinsed
15-1/4 oz. can corn, drained
14-1/2 oz. can tomatoes with
  chiles
14-1/2 oz. can diced tomatoes

14-1/2 oz. can beef broth
1 onion, chopped
1 clove garlic, minced
1-1/4 oz. pkg. taco seasoning
  mix
Garnish: sour cream, shredded
  Cheddar cheese

Combine all ingredients except garnish in a slow cooker; stir. Cover
and cook on low setting for 6 to 8 hours. Top servings with a dollop
of sour cream and sprinkle of shredded cheese. Serves 4 to 6.

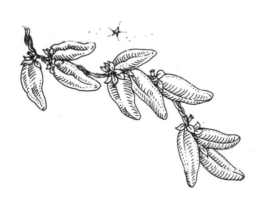

Jazz up the kitchen Tex-Mex holiday-style with
a garland of shiny dried red chile peppers!

Honey-Corn Muffins

Lisa Ann Panzino DiNunzio
Vineland, NJ

Savor these muffins on a chilly day with a steamy pot of tea...
sweetened with honey, of course!

1 c. yellow cornmeal	1/3 c. milk
1/4 c. all-purpose flour	1/4 c. corn
1-1/2 t. baking powder	1/4 c. honey
1 egg, beaten	3 T. butter, melted

Mix together cornmeal, flour and baking powder; set aside. In a separate bowl, combine egg, milk, corn, honey and butter. Add egg mixture to cornmeal mixture, stirring just enough to moisten. Fill paper-lined muffin cups 2/3 full. Bake at 400 degrees for about 20 minutes. Serve with Honey Butter. Makes 9 to 12.

Honey Butter:

1 lb. butter, softened	8-oz. jar honey

Mix together butter and honey; whip until smooth. Spoon into a covered container; keep refrigerated.

Serve up freshly baked muffins any time! Place muffins in a freezer bag and freeze. To warm frozen muffins, wrap in heavy foil and pop into a 300-degree oven for 12 to 15 minutes.

Chilly-Day *Soups*

Cincinnati-Style Chili

Jennifer Oglesby
Brownsville, IN

Living right on the Ohio border, we've come to love Cincinnati-style chili. For traditional 3-way chili, serve over cooked spaghetti and top with shredded Cheddar cheese. Top with chopped onions and cheese for a 4-way...chili beans, onions and cheese for a 5-way.

2 lbs. lean ground beef
1 qt. water
1 onion, finely chopped
8-oz. can tomato sauce
1 T. Worcestershire sauce
1 T. vinegar
1 t. garlic, minced
3 T. chili powder

2 T. allspice
3 T. ground cumin
1 t. cinnamon
1 t. celery seed
1 t. nutmeg
1 t. salt
2 bay leaves

Mix ground beef and water in a large heavy pot over medium heat. Add remaining ingredients and simmer over medium heat for 3 hours, stirring often. Discard bay leaves before serving. Makes 6 servings.

A charming welcome! Fill Victorian-style paper cones with old-fashioned hard candies and hang from chair backs with ribbons.

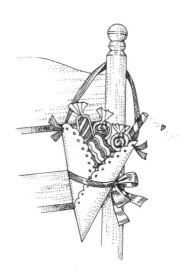

Cream of Parisian Vegetable Soup

Rita Schuette
Wauseon, OH

This is a recipe that my mom has made for years...a wonderful soup that brings back many fond memories.

1/2 lb. broccoli flowerets
1/2 lb. cauliflower flowerets
1/4 lb. carrots, peeled and sliced
2 c. water
1/2 c. butter
1/2 c. onion, chopped
1/2 c. celery, chopped

1 c. all-purpose flour
4 cubes chicken bouillon
6 c. milk
1 c. cooked ham, diced
1 t. white pepper
Optional: 1 t. flavor enhancer
salt to taste

Combine broccoli, cauliflower, carrots and water in a large soup pot over medium heat. Cook until tender; set aside, reserving liquid. Melt butter in a sauté pan over medium heat; sauté onion and celery until onion is slightly clear. Add flour; stir until well blended. Crush bouillon cubes and add to onion mixture; add milk and cooked vegetables with liquid. Cook and stir until thick and smooth. Stir in ham, pepper and flavor enhancer, if desired; add salt to taste. Simmer over low heat until hot, stirring frequently to prevent sticking. Serves 10 to 12.

Whip up a batch of napkins from cotton fabric in a cheery holiday print. Cut fabric into 12-inch squares or even 18-inch squares for lap-size napkins, then finish with a simple hem or even fringed edges...oh-so easy!

Chilly-Day *Soups*

Cauliflower-Cheddar Soup

Stacey Laliberty
Ontario, Canada

Creamy and satisfying.

2 T. butter
1/2 c. onion, chopped
3 c. cauliflower, coarsely
   chopped
10-1/2 oz. can chicken broth

2-1/2 c. milk
1/4 c. all-purpose flour
1-1/2 c. shredded Cheddar
   cheese
salt and pepper to taste

Melt butter in a large saucepan over medium heat; sauté onion until tender. Stir in cauliflower and broth; bring to a boil. Reduce heat; cover and simmer for 12 to 15 minutes, or until cauliflower is tender. Combine milk and flour until smooth; add to saucepan. Cook and stir over medium heat until boiling and thickened. Remove from heat; add cheese and stir until melted. Add salt and pepper to taste. Serves 4.

Rosemary & Onion Bread

Donna Clement
Latham, NY

My mother used to bake this bread every Sunday.
I can almost smell it now...mmm!

1 loaf frozen bread dough,
   thawed
1 to 2 T. olive oil

1 to 2 t. dried rosemary
1/4 c. onion, chopped

Coat dough with oil; place on a greased baking sheet. Press rosemary and onion into dough. Bake at 350 degrees for 30 to 40 minutes, until golden. Serves 6.

If guests will be arriving at different times, keep soup simmering in a slow cooker set on low.

Big Bad Wolf Stew

Judy Kniep
Greenfield, IA

*When my children were small, they loved the story of the three
little pigs, which ends with the wolf falling down the chimney
into the stew pot. So we always called this "Wolf Stew."*

1 lb. stew beef, cubed
3/4 c. all-purpose flour
salt and pepper to taste
3 T. oil
1 onion, thinly sliced
3 carrots, peeled and sliced
1 to 2 potatoes, peeled and
  cubed

1 t. dried thyme
2 bay leaves
12-oz. can beer or non-alcoholic
  beer
Optional: 1/4 c. flour,
  3/4 c. water

Dredge meat in flour, salt and pepper. Heat oil in a Dutch oven or soup
pot over medium heat. Brown meat lightly; remove from pot and set
aside. Add onion; cook until golden. Return meat to Dutch oven along
with carrots, potatoes, seasonings and beer. Heat to a boil, stirring
to prevent sticking. Reduce heat and simmer, covered, for one to
2 hours, stirring occasionally. Add more salt and pepper to taste, if
desired; discard bay leaves. To thicken, if desired, combine flour and
water, whisking until smooth. Gradually add to stew, stirring
constantly, until desired thickness. Serves 4 to 6.

Pass along Grandma's soup tureen or kettle to a new bride...fill it
with favorite seasonings and tie on a cherished soup recipe.

Chilly-Day *Soups*

Wallop Bread

Lesley Henry
Norfolk, VA

This recipe got its nickname because my grandmother always threatened to wallop anyone who took the beer she had set aside to make it! It is so quick & easy to make, and always takes me right back to my grandmother's kitchen.

3 c. self-rising flour
2 T. butter, melted
1/3 c. sugar

12-oz. can beer or non-alcoholic beer

Mix everything together until moistened. Pour into a greased 9"x5" loaf pan. Bake for 45 minutes at 350 degrees. Makes one loaf.

Many hands make light work, as the old saying goes, so why not invite friends to a wrapping bee? Everyone brings their gifts, tags, tape and ribbons, while you provide light snacks. With everyone helping each other, all the gifts will be wrapped in a twinkling!

Hearty Clam Chowder

Tina Marietta
Strongsville, OH

My husband and two young sons help me prepare this soup...
what a wonderful way to spend family days together!

6 slices bacon, cut into
   1/2-inch pieces
2 T. margarine
1 c. onion, chopped
10-3/4 oz. can cream of
   celery soup

1-1/2 c. milk
1-1/2 c. whipping cream
2 6-1/2 oz. cans chopped clams
5 potatoes, peeled and cut into
   1-inch cubes
Optional: 1/8 t. pepper

Partially cook bacon in a skillet over medium heat; drain. Add margarine and onion; continue cooking until onion is soft and bacon is crisp. Transfer mixture to a large saucepan; add remaining ingredients. Bring to a boil. Reduce heat and simmer for one to 1-1/2 hours, stirring occasionally. Serves 4 to 6.

The simplest centerpiece can be the prettiest. Set 2 or 3 pillar candles on an ironstone platter, then tuck vintage Christmas ornaments around the base to add sparkle.

Chilly-Day *Soups*

Creamy Garlic Soup

Sandie Cooper
Plymouth, MN

This seems like a lot of garlic and onions, but don't worry! Long,
slow cooking sweetens them, so the soup is not overpowering.
The flavor is even better the next day.

2 T. butter
2 T. olive oil
2 lbs. onions, chopped
2 c. garlic cloves, chopped
  (about 5 bulbs)
9 sprigs fresh thyme
6 sprigs fresh parsley

2 bay leaves
2 qts. regular or low-sodium
  chicken broth
1/2 loaf day-old French bread,
  cubed
2 c. half-and-half
salt and pepper to taste

Melt butter and oil in a stockpot over low heat; add onions and garlic.
Cover and cook for about 30 minutes, stirring occasionally, until very
soft and beginning to turn golden. Increase heat to medium. Continue
cooking for about 10 minutes longer until deep golden, stirring
frequently. Place herbs in a double thickness of cheesecloth; bring up
corners of cloth and tie with kitchen string to form a bag. Add broth,
bread and herb bag. Bring to a boil; reduce heat and simmer about
15 minutes. Discard herb bag; purée soup in a blender or food
processor. Pour soup back into pot through a strainer. Add half-and-
half, salt and pepper; bring back to a boil before serving. Makes
6 servings.

A favorite cook will love receiving
a gift of a soup "kit." Fill a red-
speckled enamelware soup pot
with soup bowls, oversized table
napkins and a soup ladle...
toss in a package of mini
alphabet noodles, just for fun.

Chicken Pot Pie Soup & Dumplings
Dawn Menard
Seekonk, MA

My husband works outdoors even in the winter, so for him, there's nothing like a nice hot soup with dumplings to end the day!

2 c. cooked chicken, cut into
  bite-size pieces
16-oz. pkg. frozen mixed
  vegetables
10-3/4 oz. can cream of
  potato soup
10-3/4 oz. can cream of
  chicken soup
3 c. milk, divided
2 c. biscuit baking mix

Combine chicken, vegetables, soups and 2-1/4 cups milk in a large soup pot. Bring to a boil over medium heat; reduce heat to a low simmer. Stir together baking mix and remaining milk to make a moist dough; drop into hot soup by heaping tablespoonfuls. Cook, uncovered, for 10 minutes; cover and cook another 10 minutes. Makes 4 to 6 servings.

Are the kids getting cabin fever on a snowy day? Send 'em outdoors with bottles of colored water to squirt holiday messages on the freshly fallen snow!

Chilly-Day *Soups*

Hearty Potato Soup

Teresa Potter
Branson, MO

My very own version of a wonderful soup that my husband and I used to enjoy at a special hometown restaurant.

6 potatoes, peeled and diced
1/4 c. onion, minced
salt and pepper
10-3/4 oz. can cream of celery
   soup

1 qt. milk
3 to 4 c. instant potato flakes

Place potatoes, onion, salt and pepper in a large saucepan; add enough water to cover. Bring to a boil over medium heat. Cover and cook for about 15 minutes, until potatoes are tender. Mash very lightly with a potato masher; do not drain. Add soup and mix well; add milk. When hot, stir in instant potatoes gradually until desired thickness is achieved. Simmer about 10 minutes before serving. Makes 4 servings.

One-Bowl Cheddar Biscuits

Christine Schnaufer
Geneseo, IL

These biscuits whip up oh-so quickly...they'll be eaten even quicker!

2-1/4 c. biscuit baking mix
1/2 c. shredded Cheddar cheese
2 T. fresh parsley, chopped
1/4 c. sour cream

2 T. Dijon mustard
1/3 c. milk
1 egg, beaten

Combine baking mix, cheese and parsley; stir until combined. Mix sour cream, mustard and milk in a small bowl; stir into baking mix until just combined. Place dough on a lightly floured surface; knead 10 times. Pat into a 1/2-inch thick circle; cut with a 2-inch biscuit cutter. Arrange biscuits on baking sheet; brush lightly with beaten egg. Bake at 425 degrees for 12 to 15 minutes, or until lightly golden. Serve warm. Makes 3 dozen.

Polish Mushroom & Barley Soup

Pat Stotter
Scarsdale, NY

A cup of this soup will warm you right up on a blustery day.

10 to 12 c. chicken broth
3/4 c. pearled barley, uncooked
1 onion, chopped
5 carrots, peeled and diced
4 stalks celery, diced
1/2 c. fresh parsley, divided
2 potatoes, peeled and diced
2 16-oz. pkgs. sliced
   mushrooms
salt and pepper to taste

Over medium heat, bring broth, barley and onion to a boil in a large stockpot. Stir; reduce heat and simmer for 50 minutes, stirring occasionally. Add carrots and celery and finely chopped parsley stems. Simmer an additional 15 minutes. Add potatoes and mushrooms; cook another 10 minutes, until tender. Chop parsley leaves and stir in; add salt and pepper to taste. Makes 8 to 10 servings.

When purchasing a fresh-cut Christmas tree, ask about trimmed-off branches. They're often available at little or no cost and are so handy for adding seasonal color and fresh pine scent to your home.

Chilly-Day *Soups*

Kielbasa-Cabbage Soup

Karen McCann
Marion, OH

*My son-in-law came up with this dish. It's so easy and
very tasty...real stick-to-your-ribs food for a winter day!*

1 lb. Kielbasa, halved and sliced
   into 1/4-inch pieces
28-oz. can stewed tomatoes
2 15-1/2 oz. cans dark red
   kidney beans, drained
   and rinsed
1/2 head cabbage, chopped

1 c. onion, diced
1 c. carrot, peeled and diced
1 t. pepper
6 to 8 c. chicken broth
1/2 t. dried parsley
1/2 t. dried thyme
1/2 t. dried oregano

Place Kielbasa, vegetables and pepper in a large stockpot; add broth
to cover. Bring to a boil over medium heat; cook for 20 minutes.
Reduce heat to low and continue cooking for 30 minutes, stirring
occasionally. Stir in herbs several minutes before serving. Makes 8 to
10 servings.

Chalkboard gift pots...clever holders for gifts of herb plants
or for bread sticks on the dinner table. Paint terra cotta
flowerpots with green chalkboard paint, then chalk
a holiday greeting on them. Oh-so creative!

Chicken Tortellini Soup

Karen Schmidt
Racine, WI

Savoring a bowl of this hearty soup while snuggled under a blanket watching TV...what more could you ask for on a cold winter's day?

1/4 c. butter
1/4 c. all-purpose flour
2 c. chicken broth
2 c. cooked cheese tortellini
1 c. cooked chicken, cubed

4-oz. can sliced mushrooms, drained
1 c. milk
1/2 c. grated Parmesan cheese

Melt butter in a large saucepan over medium heat. Stir flour into melted butter until smooth; add broth, tortellini, chicken and mushrooms. Simmer until thickened; add milk and Parmesan cheese. Simmer until warmed through. Serves 4 to 6.

Twisty bread sticks are a tasty go-with for soup. Brush refrigerated bread stick dough with a little beaten egg and dust with Italian seasoning, then pop in the oven until toasty. Yummy!

Chilly-Day *Soups*

Meal-in-a-Bowl Soup

Karen Augustsson
Frederick, MD

My mom was feeding a family of eight...3 girls and 3 boys, plus herself and Dad, so she would often double this recipe to accommodate all of us for dinner. You'll want to serve it with piping-hot cornbread like she did.

6 c. chicken broth
1 c. carrot, peeled and sliced
1 c. celery, sliced
1 c. frozen corn
1 c. frozen peas

1 c. cooked elbow macaroni or
    small soup pasta
2 c. cooked chicken, diced
salt and pepper to taste
1 to 2 T. fresh parsley, chopped

Pour broth into a large stockpot over medium heat; bring to a simmer. Add carrot and celery; cook until crisp-tender. Reduce heat; add remaining ingredients and simmer for approximately 30 minutes. Serves 6.

On a cozy tree-trimming night, if you're stringing
popcorn garlands, save some freshly popped corn
to enjoy as a fun soup topper.

Pumpkin-Wild Rice Soup

Jennifer Martin
Manheim, PA

My mom first served this soup on Christmas Eve several
years ago...everyone who tries this soup loves it!

1 T. butter
1 onion, diced
4 c. chicken broth
1 c. canned pumpkin

6-oz. pkg. long-grain & wild
   rice mix, prepared
1/2 c. whipping cream

Melt butter in a large saucepan over medium heat. Add onion; cook
until softened. Stir in broth, pumpkin and prepared rice. Bring to a
boil; reduce heat and add cream. Heat through, about 10 minutes.
Serves 4.

Invite friends over for a Soup Supper on a frosty winter evening.
Everyone can bring their favorite soup or bread to share...
you provide the bowls, spoons and a crackling fire!

Festive *Christmas* Dinner

Roast Fillet of Beef

Vicki Anzur
Vienna, OH

*My dad's favorite! My mother made this every Christmas Eve to serve
with shrimp cocktail, buttered parsley potatoes and a tossed salad...
a tradition that my sister and I continue with our own families.*

6-lb. fillet of beef or beef
   tenderloin, trimmed and tied
2 T. oil
2 T. mustard
1 T. Worcestershire sauce
1 T. browning and seasoning
   sauce

1 t. flavor enhancer
1/2 t. garlic salt
1 t. salt
1 t. pepper

Place beef in a large roaster pan that has been sprayed with non-stick
vegetable spray. Combine remaining ingredients and mix well; spread
over beef. Bake at 400 degrees as follows: 45 minutes for rare;
60 minutes for medium. Transfer to a serving platter and keep warm;
let stand for 15 minutes before slicing. Serves 10 to 12.

The more the merrier! Why not invite a neighbor or a college
student who might be spending the holiday alone to
share the Christmas feast?

Festive *Christmas* Dinner

Yorkshire Pudding

Patricia Murray
Ontario, Canada

*Whenever I make this recipe, I'm reminded of my mom's delicious
roast beef dinners...and sneaking back later to have
one more pudding, if there were any left!*

6 eggs
1 c. milk
1 c. all-purpose flour

1 t. salt
1/2 t. oil
drippings from roast beef

Beat together eggs and milk in a large bowl. Add flour, salt and
oil; mix well. Let rest for one hour, so mixture can come to room
temperature. Pour enough meat drippings into 24 muffin cups to
coat; place in a 450-degree oven until hot. Carefully remove tin from
oven. Pour mixture into muffin tin, filling cups a little less than half
full. Bake at 450 degrees for 16 to 18 minutes, until golden and
completely raised, being careful not to open oven door while baking.
Serve hot with roast beef and gravy. Makes 20 to 24 servings.

A bowl of colorful surprise balls doubles as a clever centerpiece
and party favors too. Wind strips of crepe paper into balls,
hiding tiny trinkets, toys, fortunes and charms between
twists of the paper. Heap the balls in a punch bowl...
what fun as the treasures are discovered!

Easiest-Ever Roast Turkey

Nancy Wysock
New Port Richey, FL

I've roasted turkeys this way for years...I even made several of these for a Thanksgiving meal at church. It's really so easy to do, and the juices that are retained in the bag make fantastic gravy.

12 to 16-lb. turkey, thawed
   if frozen
6 to 8 c. prepared stuffing
1 T. all-purpose flour
3 stalks celery

3 carrots, peeled and sliced
   lengthwise
3 onions, sliced into wedges
1/4 c. butter, softened

Rinse turkey and pat dry. Lightly stuff turkey with stuffing and set aside. Place flour in a roasting bag and shake to coat. Arrange vegetables in the bottom of bag. Place turkey in bag on top of vegetables; rub turkey with softened butter. Close bag with tie provided; cut six, 1/2-inch slits in top of bag. Place turkey in a roasting pan. Roast turkey at 350 degrees for 2-1/2 to 3 hours, until a meat thermometer inserted in thickest part of thigh reads 165 degrees. Let turkey rest for about 15 minutes before carving. Serves 10 to 12.

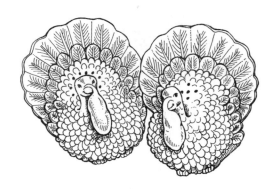

Tomorrow is the big day and the turkey is still frozen solid!
Place it in a large cooler and cover with cold water,
changing the water once an hour. A 12 to
14-pound bird will thaw in about 8 hours.

Grandmother's Oyster Stuffing

Patricia Kuhn
Goshen, IN

Since oysters were expensive, my grandmother only made this stuffing once a year as a special treat. The house would be so packed with relatives we could hardly move, and all the "girls" would be in the kitchen helping Grandma make her stuffing. Such memories!

1 loaf bread, torn
neck, liver and gizzard of
   roasting turkey
1/2 c. butter
1/2 c. onion, minced
1/2 c. celery, chopped

2 t. dried sage
2 t. salt, or to taste
1/4 t. pepper
3 eggs, beaten
1 pt. fresh oysters, drained

Place bread in a large 2-quart bowl; set aside. Place turkey neck, liver and gizzard in a medium saucepan; add water to cover and simmer over medium heat until cooked. In a separate saucepan, melt butter. Add onion, celery, sage, salt and pepper; cook until vegetables are tender. Add butter mixture to bread and stir together. Add eggs to bread mixture and gently toss until blended. Reserving the cooking broth, pull meat off turkey neck; break up liver and gizzard. Add to bread mixture. Pour reserved broth over bread until moist; gently mix in oysters. Makes about 8 cups, enough to stuff a 20-pound turkey. Serves 6 to 8.

Cut snowflakes from folded paper, then scatter your creations around the dining table...how delightful!

Green Pea Casserole

Norma Still
Punta Gorda, FL

A tasty twist on the familiar green bean bake.

2 10-oz. pkgs. frozen peas,
    cooked and drained
10-3/4 oz. can cream of
    mushroom soup

1 c. shredded Cheddar cheese
1 c. French fried onions

Stir together peas and soup. Spoon mixture into a greased 9" deep-dish pie plate; sprinkle with cheese. Bake at 350 degrees for 20 to 25 minutes. Remove from oven; top with onions. Return to oven for about 5 minutes. Makes 4 to 6 servings.

Honey-Thyme Veggies

Phyllis Adolph
Roundup, MT

A few simple ingredients wake up plain veggies in a snap.

16-oz. pkg. frozen California-
    style vegetables
2 T. butter, melted

2 T. honey
1/4 t. dried thyme

Cook vegetables according to package directions. Drain; stir in remaining ingredients. Serves 4.

Tuck family photos on wire picks into an evergreen arrangement...a clever conversation starter for holiday guests.

Festive *Christmas* Dinner

Cheddar Potato Gratin

Vickie
Gooseberry Patch

Everyone's favorite cheesy potatoes, but extra special for the holidays.

2 t. dried sage
1-1/2 t. salt
1/2 t. pepper
3 lbs. potatoes, peeled, thinly
    sliced and divided
1 onion, thinly sliced and
    divided

8-oz. pkg. shredded Cheddar
    cheese, divided
1 c. whipping cream
1 c. chicken broth

Mix sage, salt and pepper in a cup; set aside. Layer one-third of
potatoes and half of onion in a lightly greased 13"x9" baking pan.
Sprinkle with one teaspoon of sage mixture and one-third of cheese.
Repeat layers with remaining ingredients, ending with cheese. Whisk
cream and broth together until well blended; pour evenly over top.
Bake, covered, at 400 degrees for one hour, until tender and golden.
Let stand 5 minutes before serving. Makes 10 to 12 servings.

Looking for a new garnish for roasts, soups and potato
casseroles? Try some tasty fried sage! Drop fresh sage leaves,
a few at a time, into a skillet of hot oil. Fry for just a few
seconds until leaves are crisp and bright green; remove with
tongs. Drain on a paper towel and sprinkle with salt.

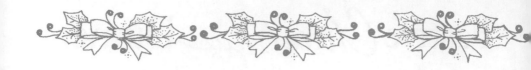

Sweet Potato Meringue

Jill Valentine
Jackson, TN

At Christmas dinner, we take a few moments for everyone to share their blessings. Uncle Fred always gets a laugh by saying, "Thank goodness Great-Grandma brought the Sweet Potato Meringue again!"

2 c. canned sweet potatoes,
    drained and mashed
1/3 c. plus 2 T. sugar, divided
1 t. vanilla extract
1/2 t. cinnamon
1/4 t. nutmeg

2 c. milk
4 eggs, divided
1/2 c. golden raisins
1/2 c. sweetened flaked coconut
1/3 c. orange marmalade

In a large bowl, combine sweet potatoes, 1/3 cup sugar, vanilla and spices; set aside. Beat one whole egg, 3 egg yolks and milk; stir into mixture. Add raisins and coconut; spoon into a greased 2-1/2 quart casserole dish. Bake, uncovered, at 400 degrees for 35 minutes, stirring after 15 minutes. Remove from oven. Warm marmalade in a small saucepan; spread over casserole. In a small bowl, with an electric mixer on high speed, beat reserved egg whites till soft peaks form. Gradually add remaining sugar, beating till stiff peaks form. Spoon mixture around edges of casserole. Return to oven; bake an additional 5 to 6 minutes, or until meringue is golden. Let stand 30 minutes before serving. Serve warm. Makes 6 to 8 servings.

Set a teeny-tiny snowman at each person's place...so cute! Simply glue white pompoms together with craft glue, then add faces and scarves clipped from bits of felt.

Festive *Christmas* Dinner

Homemade Potato Biscuits

Linda Cuellar
Riverside, CA

These are wonderful right out of the oven. Great with butter, jam or apple butter...did I mention honey? Truly a comfort food.

1/2 c. instant potato flakes	1/2 c. hot water
1 t. sugar	1/3 c. cold water
2 T. butter, softened	2 c. biscuit baking mix

Stir together instant potato flakes, sugar, butter and hot water; stir in cold water and baking mix. Gently smooth dough into a ball on a floured board; knead 8 to 10 times. Roll out dough into a 10-inch by 6-inch rectangle; cut into 12 squares. Arrange on an ungreased baking sheet. Bake at 450 degrees for about 10 minutes, until golden. Serve warm. Makes one dozen.

Christmas tree farms sometimes offer rides in horse-drawn sleighs or wagons...take the family for a ride they'll never forget! Tuck in a thermos of hot cocoa for warming up along the way.

Spinach & Clementine Salad

Sharon Jones
Oklahoma City, OK

*This fresh, crunchy salad is a perfect way to use
a Christmas gift box of clementines.*

2 lbs. clementines, peeled and
   sectioned
2 lbs. baby spinach
4 stalks celery, thinly sliced on
   the diagonal
1 c. red onion, thinly sliced
1/2 c. pine nuts or walnuts,
   toasted

1/4 c. dried cherries
2 T. red wine vinegar
1/4 c. olive oil
1 t. Dijon mustard
1 clove garlic, minced
1/8 t. sugar
salt and pepper to taste

Place clementines in a large salad bowl with spinach, celery, onion,
nuts and cherries. Toss to mix well. Whisk together remaining
ingredients in a small bowl; drizzle over salad. Serve immediately.
Makes 8 servings.

Sprinkle a tossed green salad with ruby-red
pomegranate seeds for a festive touch.

Festive *Christmas* Dinner

Country-Style Rice Dressing

Mary Ann Dell
Phoenixville, PA

Oh-so easy to make...equally good with roast turkey, pork or beef.

2 c. water
1 c. long-cooking brown rice,
  uncooked
1/4 lb. ground pork or turkey
  sausage
3 c. sliced mushrooms
1 c. onion, chopped

3/4 c. carrot, peeled and
  shredded
1/2 c. sweetened dried
  cranberries
1/4 c. fresh parsley, chopped
2 T. fresh basil, chopped
salt and pepper to taste

Bring water to a boil in a saucepan. Stir in rice; cover and simmer over low heat for 20 to 25 minutes, or until tender. In a large skillet over medium heat, cook sausage, mushrooms and onion until sausage is brown and vegetables are tender. Drain; stir in carrot, cranberries and herbs. Stir cooked rice into sausage mixture; add salt and pepper to taste. Cook and stir until heated through. Makes 8 servings.

For a sparkly candle in a jiffy, pin shiny gold sequins in
a starburst shape on a chunky red pillar candle.

Baked Cola Ham

Jennifer Oglesby
Brownsville, IN

I love to take this ham to church socials and family get-togethers...
there are never any leftovers!

12 to 15-lb. fully-cooked
   bone-in ham
1 t. allspice

2-ltr. bottle cola
3/4 c. cherry jelly
1/4 c. orange juice

Trim rind and any excess fat from ham, leaving a 1/4-inch thick
layer of fat. Place ham in an ungreased roasting pan. Score fat into a
diamond pattern; sprinkle with allspice and rub into ham. Pour cola
into roasting pan. Bake, uncovered, at 325 degrees for one hour and
15 minutes, basting every 15 minutes with pan juices. Combine jelly
and orange juice in a small saucepan. Cook and stir over medium heat
until melted; brush over top and sides of ham. Return ham to oven.
Continue baking for 15 to 30 minutes, basting every 15 minutes,
until a meat thermometer inserted into thickest part of ham registers
140 degrees. Let ham rest for 30 minutes to one hour before slicing.
Makes 16 to 20 servings.

Don't save them for "someday," make some memories now...
go ahead and use Grandma's best china and silver!

Festive *Christmas* Dinner

Creamed Peas & Onions

Amy Kim
Ann Arbor, MI

Our new favorite way to enjoy peas...it's so simple but so yummy!

1/4 c. butter
1/4 c. all-purpose flour
1-1/2 c. milk
16-oz. pkg. frozen peas and
    onions, thawed

1 t. onion powder
salt and pepper to taste

Melt butter in a large skillet over low heat; stir in flour until smooth. Increase heat to medium and stir in milk, 1/2 cup at a time, until thickened. Stir in peas and onions; add onion powder, salt and pepper. Heat through and serve. Makes 4 to 6 servings.

Granny Margaret's Carrots

Polly McCallum
Pulatka, FL

Everything always tastes better at Granny's. My kids love these carrots, but when I make them, they say they're not like Granny's!

16-oz. pkg. baby carrots
1 T. butter
1/4 c. brown sugar, packed

1/4 c. orange juice
1/2 t. salt

Cover carrots with water in a medium saucepan. Cook over medium heat until carrots are tender, about 15 minutes; drain. Stir in remaining ingredients. Heat until warmed through. Serves 6.

A cheery welcome at the front door! Tie a bundle of evergreen clippings to a rustic twig broom with a jaunty red bow.

Christmas Ribbon Salad

Vicki Holland
Hampton, GA

This tricolored gelatin salad may seem complicated, but it isn't! Just follow along step-by-step and before you know it, you're done.

8-1/2 oz. can crushed pineapple, drained and syrup reserved
3-oz. pkg. lime gelatin mix
8-oz. pkg. cream cheese, softened
1/2 c. sugar
1 c. evaporated milk

1 t. vanilla extract
1 env. unflavored gelatin
1/4 c. cold water
3-oz. pkg. strawberry gelatin mix
10-oz. pkg. frozen strawberries, thawed, drained and syrup reserved

For green layer, place pineapple in an ungreased 8"x8" clear glass baking pan. Add enough water to reserved pineapple syrup to equal 1-1/4 cups. Heat to boiling; dissolve lime gelatin in hot liquid. Pour over pineapple; chill until firm. For white layer, beat cream cheese with sugar until soft and smooth. Gradually blend in evaporated milk and vanilla. Soften unflavored gelatin in 1/4 cup cold water and heat to dissolve. Blend into cream cheese mixture and pour over lime layer; chill until very firm. For red layer, add enough water to reserved strawberry syrup to equal 1-1/4 cups. Heat to boiling; dissolve strawberry gelatin in hot liquid. Stir in strawberries; cool to room temperature. Carefully spoon strawberry mixture over cream cheese layer; chill until firm. Cut into squares. Makes 10 servings.

Wind strands of glossy red wooden beads around a holiday buffet or evergreen wreath. They're as decorative as fresh cranberries, yet can be packed away to re-use next year.

Festive *Christmas* Dinner

Waldorf Slaw

Lori Rosenberg
University Heights, OH

A tangy salad that's easily made ahead.

16-oz. pkg. coleslaw mix
2 c. Braeburn apples, cored,
   peeled and chopped
1 c. Bartlett pears, cored, peeled
   and chopped
1/2 c. raisins
3 T. chopped walnuts

1/2 c. mayonnaise
1/2 c. buttermilk
1 t. lemon zest
2 T. lemon juice
1/4 t. salt
1/8 t. pepper

Combine coleslaw mix, apples, pears, raisins and walnuts in a large bowl; set aside. Combine remaining ingredients, stirring well with a whisk. Drizzle mayonnaise mixture over coleslaw mixture and toss to coat. Cover and refrigerate 30 minutes. Makes 10 servings.

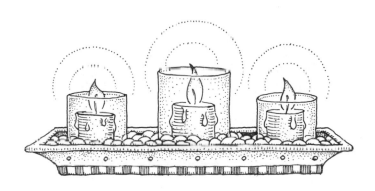

Set lighted votives on a shallow tray filled with glass pebbles for a quick & easy centerpiece.

Sweet Onion & Swiss Casserole
Virginia King Hugill
Woodinville, WA

A tried & true favorite from my great-aunt, Laura Selman Goodley.

2 c. sweet onions, thinly sliced
2 c. shredded Swiss cheese
1 c. mayonnaise

1/4 t. dill weed
1/4 t. celery salt
1/4 t. white pepper

Place all ingredients in a large bowl and mix well. Spoon into a lightly greased 1-1/2 quart casserole dish. Bake, uncovered, at 350 degrees for 30 minutes, or until cheese is bubbly and golden on top. Serves 4.

Arrange evergreen clippings in the bottom of a glass trifle bowl. Fill the bowl with shiny red ornaments and add sparkly strands of beads around the bowl's edges...an easy centerpiece.

Festive *Christmas* Dinner

Grammy's Beef Brisket

Sarah Blasi
Iuka, KS

When I got married, Grammy gave me a recipe organizer filled with some of her favorites. This recipe brings back great memories of family holidays, get-togethers and even the dinner at our wedding reception!

4-lb. flat-cut beef brisket
2 t. salt
1/2 t. pepper
1 clove garlic, minced

3 onions, thickly sliced
1 c. hot water
2 T. cornstarch
1 c. cold water

Place brisket flat-side up in an ungreased roasting pan. Sprinkle with salt, pepper and garlic; add onions. Bake, uncovered, at 350 degrees for one hour, or until onions turn lightly golden. Add hot water to pan; cover pan tightly with aluminum foil. Reduce oven to 300 degrees and continue baking for an additional 2 hours. Remove brisket and onions to a warm serving platter. To make gravy, combine cornstarch and cold water; stir into juices in roasting pan. Place pan on burner on top of stove and cook until gravy thickens, stirring constantly. Serves 10 to 12.

A Christmas family party...we know of nothing in nature more delightful! There seems a magic in the very name of Christmas.
– Charles Dickens

Marinated Veggie Salad

Lanita Anderson
Chesapeake, VA

This recipe is from my grandmother, who made it every year to go along with her Thanksgiving and Christmas dinners. Now that she's in her 90's, I am happy to do the cooking for her.

1/2 c. oil
3/4 c. vinegar
1 c. sugar
1 t. salt
1 t. pepper
14-1/2 oz. can French-style
   green beans, drained
15-1/4 oz. can green peas,
   drained

15-oz. can shoepeg corn,
   drained
15-1/4 oz. can yellow corn,
   drained
2-oz. jar chopped pimentos,
   drained
1 green pepper, diced
1 white or red onion, diced
1 c. celery, diced

To make marinade, combine oil, vinegar, sugar, salt and pepper in a small saucepan. Bring to a boil; remove from heat and let cool. Combine vegetables in a large bowl. Pour cooled marinade over vegetables and mix well. Chill in refrigerator for at least 2 hours before serving; best if chilled overnight. Makes 10 to 12 servings.

A heavenly host! Round up sweet angel figures to place on a cloud of fluffy angel hair along a mantel.

Festive *Christmas* Dinner

Brandied Cranberries

Robin Dennis
Vernonia, OR

Family & friends look forward to this spirited cranberry relish at our holiday dinners.

12-oz. pkg. cranberries
2 c. sugar

1/2 c. brandy

Combine ingredients in a lightly greased 1-1/2 quart casserole dish. Cover and bake at 300 degrees for 45 minutes. Stir several times while baking. Refrigerate overnight; serve warm or cold. Serves 5.

Carrot Soufflé

Mary Rabon
Mobile, AL

My children, Gabrielle and Jonathan, snub most vegetables yet absolutely adore this! Enjoy it as a side dish or even a dessert.

3 lbs. carrots, peeled and sliced
2 c. sugar
1 T. baking powder
1 T. vanilla extract

1/4 c. all-purpose flour
6 eggs, beaten
1 c. butter, softened
Optional: powdered sugar

Cover carrots with water in a medium saucepan. Cook over medium heat until tender and soft. Drain well; add sugar, baking powder and vanilla. Beat with an electric mixer on low speed until smooth. Add flour and mix well; add eggs and blend well. Stir in butter. Pour into a lightly greased 13"x9" baking pan. Bake, uncovered, at 350 degrees for about one hour, or until golden. Sprinkle lightly with powdered sugar, if desired. Makes 10 servings.

Tourtière

Kim Trode
Pennellville, NY

This French-Canadian meat pie has been a Christmastime tradition in my family for a long time. This recipe comes from my dear Mémère (French for Gramma), Hortense Robidoux. She passed it along to my mother, Louise Sherry, who in turn shared it with me. We enjoy it served with cranberry sauce and gravy from the Christmas turkey.

2 9-inch pie crusts
1/2 lb. ground beef
1/2 lb. ground pork
1 clove garlic, minced
1 stalk celery, finely chopped
1 carrot, peeled and finely
    chopped
3/4 c. plus 1 t. water, divided

3 cubes chicken bouillon
1 bay leaf
1/4 t. pepper
1/4 t. cinnamon
1/8 t. nutmeg
1/8 t. ground cloves
1 potato, peeled and grated
1 egg yolk

Place one pie crust in a 9" pie plate and set aside. Mix ground meats, garlic, celery, carrot, 3/4 cup water, bouillon and seasonings in a skillet. Cook and stir over medium heat for 7 to 8 minutes, until meat is no longer pink; drain. Remove bay leaf; add potato and spoon meat mixture into pie plate. Place top crust over mixture and press edges to seal; crimp and vent. Mix egg yolk and remaining water together; brush over top crust. Bake at 375 degrees for 30 to 40 minutes, until golden. Serves 6 to 8.

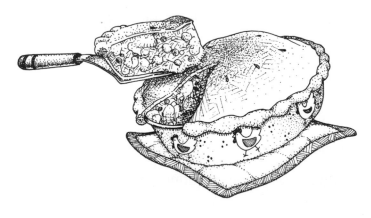

Festive *Christmas* Dinner

Garlic Scalloped Potatoes

Penny Sherman
Cumming, GA

Almost as good as Mom's, but really easy to fix!

19-oz. can chunky-style creamy
   potato soup with roasted
   garlic
1/2 c. whipping cream
1/2 c. water
1 t. dried thyme
1 t. pepper
6 potatoes, peeled, sliced
   and divided
2-1/2 c. shredded Cheddar
   cheese, divided

Combine soup, cream, water and seasonings in a blender; process until smooth. Spread half of soup mixture in a lightly greased 13"x9" baking pan. Arrange half of potatoes in pan; sprinkle with 2 cups cheese. Top with remaining potatoes; spread remaining soup mixture over top. Sprinkle with remaining cheese. Bake, uncovered, at 350 degrees for 35 minutes. Cover and continue to bake for an additional 35 minutes, until hot and bubbly. Serves 8.

Take the kids to a paint-your-own pottery shop.
They'll love decorating a plate and mug
especially for Santa's milk and cookies!

Fluffy French Bread Stuffing

Rachel Meinert
Shelby Township, MI

*Our family can't get enough of this sage-flavored stuffing at
Christmas...I usually have to make two batches!*

8 c. soft French bread, cubed
1 c. saltine crackers, crushed
1 t. dried sage
1 c. onion, chopped
1/2 c. celery, chopped

1/2 c. butter
10-3/4 oz. cream of chicken
   soup
2 eggs, beaten
1/4 c. fresh parsley, chopped

Combine bread cubes, cracker crumbs and sage in a large bowl; set
aside. In a skillet over medium heat, cook onion and celery in butter
until tender. Pour onion mixture over bread mixture. Add soup, eggs
and parsley; toss lightly. Makes enough to stuff a 6 to 8-pound turkey
or two, 3 to 4-pound chickens. Can also be placed in a lightly greased
4-quart casserole dish; cover with aluminum foil and bake at
350 degrees for one hour. Makes 8 servings.

To keep a potted Christmas poinsettia fresh, place it
in a sunny spot, away from cold drafts. Water
whenever the soil on top feels dry.

Festive *Christmas* Dinner

Pineapple-Cranberry Pork Roast

Carrie Kelderman
Pella, IA

A family-favorite way to enjoy pork roast during the holidays.

3-lb. pork loin roast	1 c. sweetened dried cranberries
20-oz. can crushed pineapple	2 T. all-purpose flour
1.35-oz. pkg. onion soup mix	3 T. water

Place roast in a slow cooker. In a bowl, mix together pineapple with juice, soup mix and cranberries; spoon mixture over roast. Cover and cook on low setting for 8 hours. Remove roast to a serving platter and increase heat to high setting. In a cup, mix together flour and water; whisk into juices in slow cooker. Cook for 15 minutes, or until gravy has thickened. Serve pork drizzled with gravy from slow cooker. Serves 6 to 8.

Perfectly personal...wouldn't grandparents, aunts & uncles just love a family photo calendar? Pick out a dozen sweet, funny and memorable snapshots for the neighborhood copy shop to turn into printed calendars...birthdays and other special dates can even be added.

Yellow Bowl Cloverleaf Rolls

Monica Wilkinson
Burton, SC

This recipe has been popular in our family for four generations! My mom remembers my grandma making these in a yellow mixing bowl. Mom continued that tradition and made hers in a yellow bowl too... I can still see the dough rising up over the top in the refrigerator.

1 c. warm water	4 t. salt
2 envs. active dry yeast	2/3 c. oil
3/4 c. plus 1 t. sugar, divided	2 eggs, beaten
2 c. warm milk	10 to 11 c. all-purpose flour

Pour warm water, about 110 to 115 degrees, into a large bowl. Add yeast and one teaspoon sugar; stir to dissolve. Mix in milk, salt, remaining sugar and oil. Add eggs, beating well. Add enough flour to make a soft dough; let stand for 10 minutes. Knead until smooth and elastic, adding flour as needed. Place in a large greased bowl; cover with a tea towel and refrigerate overnight. Spray muffin tins with non-stick vegetable spray. Shape dough into one-inch balls; place 3 balls into each muffin cup. Cover; let rise until double in bulk. Bake at 400 degrees for 15 to 20 minutes. Makes about 3-1/2 dozen.

Cinnamon Rolls:

Follow above recipe. Roll out refrigerated dough to an 18-inch by 12-inch rectangle. 1/2 cup softened butter to within one inch of long edges. Sprinkle with 1-1/2 cups brown sugar, 6 tablespoons cinnamon and 1-1/2 cups chopped walnuts. Roll up dough; seal edges. Using a sharp knife, cut rolls into one-inch slices and place 6 rolls each in lightly greased 8" round cake pans. Cover; let rise until double in bulk. Bake at 350 degrees until golden, about 15 minutes. Combine 2 cups powdered sugar and 2 tablespoons milk to form a glaze; drizzle over warm rolls. Serve warm. Makes about 3-1/2 dozen.

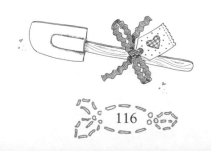

Festive *Christmas* Dinner

Dijon Garden Casserole

Amanda Lusignolo
Westerville, OH

For a crunchy topping, sprinkle with crushed herb-flavored stuffing before slipping this savory dish into the oven.

2 c. broccoli, chopped
2 c. cauliflower, chopped
2 c. onion, chopped
1 c. shredded sharp Cheddar
   cheese
1 c. mayonnaise

3 T. Dijon mustard
1/2 t. salt
1/4 t. pepper
2 cloves garlic, pressed
1 t. dried parsley

Steam or boil vegetables separately until crisp-tender; drain well. Layer half each of broccoli, cauliflower and onion in a lightly greased 2-quart casserole dish; repeat layering with remaining vegetables. Combine remaining ingredients; spread over top. Bake, uncovered, at 350 degrees for 20 minutes, until bubbly. Makes 6 to 8 servings.

A kitchen wreath looks festive decorated with cookie cutters, nutmeg graters, honey dippers and mini kitchen tools.

Maple-Glazed Chicken & Yams

Kathy Grashoff
Fort Wayne, IN

Substitute your favorite fresh herb if you like...rosemary and tarragon are perfect partners with chicken too.

4-lb. chicken, cut into
  serving-size pieces
1 yellow onion, sliced into
  wedges
2 yams or sweet potatoes,
  peeled and cubed

2 T. olive oil
1 t. salt
1/4 t. pepper
3 T. maple syrup
6 sprigs fresh thyme

Arrange chicken, onion and yams or sweet potatoes in a lightly greased 13"x9" baking pan. Drizzle with oil; sprinkle with salt and pepper and toss to coat. Drizzle with syrup; top with thyme. Bake, uncovered, at 400 degrees for about one hour and 15 minutes, stirring vegetables once, until chicken juices run clear. Let stand for 10 minutes before serving. Serves 4.

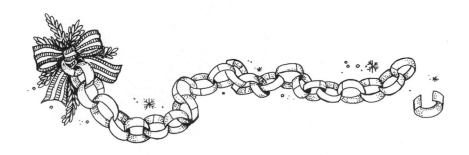

Make a happiness chain to wind around the tree. Cut strips of colorful paper and have family members write a few words on each strip about what makes them feel happy..."my cat Fluffy," "making snow angels" and so on. Tape strips together into loops to form a chain...sure to bring smiles!

Festive *Christmas* Dinner

Pineapple Casserole

Faith Deaton
Southaven, MS

I first met my future mother-in-law on Christmas Eve. I was included in the family Christmas celebration which of course included a large Christmas dinner. She served this recipe of pineapple casserole which was and is a family favorite. It is now served at both Thanksgiving and Christmas for both my husband's family and mine.

1/2 c. sugar
3 T. all-purpose flour
1 c. shredded Cheddar cheese
20-oz. can pineapple chunks,
    drained and 3 T. juice
    reserved

1/2 c. round buttery crackers,
    crushed
1/4 c. butter, melted

Stir together sugar and flour in a large bowl; gradually stir in cheese. Add pineapple; mix well. Spoon into a buttered 1-1/2 quart casserole dish. In a separate bowl, combine cracker crumbs, melted butter and reserved pineapple juice. until well blended. Sprinkle cracker mixture over pineapple mixture. Bake, uncovered, at 350 degrees for 20 to 30 minutes, until golden. Serves 4.

Quickly turn a group of mismatched tag-sale candleholders into a shimmering set...spray them all your favorite color of craft paint. All white or ivory looks snowy tucked among evergreen and holiday decorations.

Savory Garlic Chicken

Cathy Hillier
Salt Lake City, UT

A cozy meal just for the two of you!

4 cloves garlic, sliced
2 T. butter
2 boneless, skinless chicken
  breasts
1/2 t. salt
1/2 t. pepper

1 onion, sliced
2 whole cloves
1 bay leaf
1 c. white wine or chicken broth
1/2 c. sour cream
Optional: cooked rice

In a skillet over medium heat, sauté garlic in butter just until golden; remove garlic from skillet. Sauté chicken until golden on both sides, about 7 minutes. Sprinkle with salt and pepper; remove from skillet. Add onion, cloves and bay leaf to skillet. Return chicken and garlic to skillet; drizzle with wine or broth. Reduce heat; cover and simmer for 15 to 20 minutes, until juices run clear. Remove chicken from skillet; keep warm while making sauce. Increase heat to medium; cook and stir pan juices until reduced to about 1/2 cup. Discard cloves and bay leaf. Add sour cream; cook and stir until warmed through. Spoon sauce over chicken; serve with cooked rice, if desired. Serves 2.

A real conversation starter...ask older relatives about their earliest holiday memories. Did they have a Christmas tree? How was it decorated? Do they recall setting out cookies & milk for Santa? Don't miss the opportunity to preserve these precious memories on video.

Festive *Christmas* Dinner

Greek Spinach

Kathy Walstrom
Glenview, IL

Our family loves this Greek side dish...it's a recipe that my grandmother (Yiayia in Greek) made all the time. We like to add a little feta cheese and fresh lemon after it's cooked...heavenly!

1/3 c. olive oil
2 onions, chopped
2 lbs. spinach
8-oz. can tomato sauce
2 c. water

1 t. dill weed
1 t. dried parsley
salt and pepper to taste
1/2 c. long-cooking white rice, uncooked

Heat oil in a large skillet over medium-high heat; sauté onions until soft and translucent. Add spinach and cook, stirring, for a few minutes; pour in tomato sauce and water. Bring to a boil; sprinkle with dill weed, parsley, salt and pepper. Stir in uncooked rice; reduce heat to low. Simmer, uncovered, for 20 to 25 minutes, or until rice is tender, adding more water if necessary. Makes 4 to 6 servings.

Set out a guest book when guests come to dinner!
Ask everyone young and old to sign...it will become
a treasured journal of the holiday.

Uncle's Cornbread Dressing

Gayle Baskin
Paso Robles, CA

This recipe was originally my uncle's...I've been making it every Thanksgiving and Christmas for 44 years now!

15-oz. pkg. cornbread mix
12-oz. pkg. stuffing mix
3/4 c. butter, melted and divided
1 onion, diced
4 stalks celery, diced
1 t. salt
1 t. pepper

2 8-oz. cans chicken broth
1 t. dried sage
1 t. poultry seasoning
1 bay leaf
1 c. golden raisins
1 egg, beaten

Bake cornbread as directed on package; let cool. Crumble on a baking sheet and bake at 200 degrees until dry and crispy, about 2 hours. Toss cornbread with stuffing mix and seasoning packet in a large bowl; set aside. Pour 1/2 cup butter into a large skillet. Sauté onion and celery until translucent; sprinkle with salt and pepper. Add broth and remaining seasonings to skillet; simmer over low heat until heated through. Remove bay leaf. Add onion mixture to cornbread mixture, stirring to moisten completely; gently stir in raisins. Just before baking, stir in egg. Spoon stuffing into a buttered 13"x9" baking pan; drizzle with remaining butter. Bake, uncovered, at 350 degrees for 30 minutes, until heated through and golden on top. Makes 8 to 12 servings.

Whip up a batch of drawstring bags in cheery Christmas-print fabric for no-fuss gift wrapping...just pop in a gift and tie the strings in a bow. They'll be reusable year after year too.

Festive *Christmas* Dinner

Cheesy Garlic Biscuits

Lisa Ann Panzino DiNunzio
Vineland, NJ

When I first made these biscuits, everyone at our church fellowship lunch simply raved about them! The garlic and parsley butter brushed over them is just the perfect match for these tender biscuits...I am sure I will be making them again & again!

1-1/4 c. biscuit baking mix
1/2 c. shredded Cheddar cheese
1/2 c. water

1/4 c. butter, melted
1/4 t. garlic powder
1/4 t. dried parsley

Combine baking mix and cheese in a small bowl. Add water and stir just until combined and slightly moistened. Drop dough by tablespoonfuls onto baking sheets that have been lightly sprayed with non-stick vegetable spray. Bake at 400 degrees for about 10 minutes, or until firm and beginning to turn golden. Combine remaining ingredients in a small bowl; mix well. As soon as biscuits come out of oven, brush them with butter mixture using a pastry brush. Serve warm. Makes about one dozen.

When setting a children's table for Christmas dinner, make it playful! Cover the tabletop with giftwrap, decorate paper cups and napkins with holiday stickers and add a gingerbread house centerpiece...the kids will beg to sit there!

Creamy Mushroom Chicken

Jackie Furia Lau
Willits, CA

Elegant enough for company, yet oh-so simple to prepare.
Sprinkle with chopped fresh parsley before serving.

1 lb. boneless, skinless chicken
  breast, cubed
1-1/4 oz. pkg. chicken
  gravy mix
10-3/4 oz. can cream of
  mushroom soup

1 c. white wine or chicken broth
8-oz. pkg. cream cheese, cubed
cooked pasta or rice

Place chicken in a slow cooker. Sprinkle gravy mix over chicken;
add soup and wine or broth. Cover and cook on low setting for 5 to
6 hours. Add cream cheese 30 minutes before serving. Remove
chicken from slow cooker; vigorously whisk sauce. Serve chicken
and sauce over hot, cooked pasta or rice. Makes 4 to 6 servings.

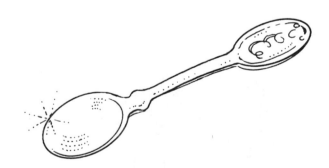

Gleaming silver looks sparkly on a candlelit dining table.
Use this easy trick to quickly remove tarnish. Lay a strip of
aluminum foil in a kitchen basin, fill with water and add
2 tablespoons salt. Place silver in the basin...in just
2 to 3 minutes, it will be ready to rinse and dry.

Festive *Christmas* Dinner

Golden Potato Latkes

Irene Robinson
Cincinnati, OH

Enjoy these tasty potato pancakes the traditional way,
topped with applesauce and a dollop of sour cream.

4 baking potatoes, peeled	1 t. salt
1 onion	1/2 t. pepper
1/4 c. all-purpose flour	3/4 c. oil
4 eggs, beaten	

Shred potatoes and onion in a food processor; transfer to a large bowl.
Stir in flour, eggs, salt and pepper until blended. Heat oil in a large
skillet over medium-high heat. Drop potato mixture into hot oil,
2 tablespoons at a time. Cook over medium-high heat, turning once,
until golden. Drain on paper towels; serve warm. Makes about
one dozen.

Look for retro photo frames at flea markets and tag sales...
they'll look charming with snapshots from Christmases past.

Fire & Spice Baked Ham

Linda Belon
Wintersville, OH

Is there anything more taste-tempting than the aroma of a baked ham?
We don't think so! Make it the star of a festive holiday meal,
then savor the leftovers as ham sandwiches.

5-1/2 to 6-lb. fully-cooked
   ham half
1/2 c. red pepper jelly

1/2 c. pineapple preserves
1/4 c. brown sugar, packed
1/4 t. ground cloves

Trim off rind and excess fat from ham; score fat in a diamond pattern.
Place ham on a broiler pan sprayed with non-stick vegetable spray.
Combine remaining ingredients in a small saucepan over low heat,
stirring with a whisk until well blended. Brush one-third of jelly
mixture over ham; bake at 425 degrees for 5 minutes. Turn down
oven temperature to 325 degrees. Bake ham, uncovered, for an
additional 45 minutes, basting with remaining jelly mixture every
15 minutes. Transfer ham to a serving platter; let stand for 15 minutes
before slicing. Makes 8 to 10 servings.

Punch holes at the top of vintage alphabet flashcards
and thread onto a ribbon to spell out holiday wishes.

Festive *Christmas* Dinner

Cranberry Dream Salad

Marsha Sherbert
Cowpens, SC

This recipe is a big hit around Thanksgiving, and Christmas!
It is sweet enough to be a dessert or a side.

12-oz. pkg. cranberries
2 c. sugar
20-oz. can crushed pineapple
8-oz. pkg. mini marshmallows

1 banana, sliced
1 c. frozen whipped topping,
  thawed

Grind cranberries in a food processor or blender. Add sugar, crushed pineapple and marshmallows; spoon into a large bowl. Chill overnight in refrigerator. Just before serving, fold in banana and whipped topping. Makes 10 to 12 servings.

Bring out Grandma's whimsical Christmas table linens for family gatherings. Decorated with smiling Santas or bright poinsettias, they're sure to spark fun memories.

Thyme-Roasted Potatoes

Kathleen Sturm
Corona, CA

My step-grandmother, Melba, made these for Christmas one year.
I had to have the recipe before leaving that night...oh-so good!

4 cloves garlic, peeled
2 t. salt
2 T. fresh thyme, minced
2 T. olive oil

1-1/2 to 2 lbs. new redskin
　potatoes, halved or quartered
pepper to taste

In a small bowl, mash garlic and salt together to make a coarse paste.
Mix in thyme; slowly pour in oil and blend thoroughly. Place potatoes
in a large bowl. Pour garlic mixture over potatoes and toss to coat.
Place in a large ungreased roasting pan; sprinkle with pepper to taste.
Cover with aluminum foil; bake at 375 degrees for 50 minutes.
Uncover and allow to bake 15 to 20 minutes longer, until tender
and lightly golden. Makes 6 to 8 servings.

Turn old glass ornaments into shiny new ones with
a squeeze bottle of gold or silver glitter paint. Decorate
with swirls, dots or even names...it's so easy!

Chocolate Eggnog, page 55

One-Bowl Cheddar Biscuits, page 87

Pepper Jack–Crab Bisque, page 74

Brie Kisses, page 9

Spinach & Clementine Salad, page 102

Zesty Brunch Quiche, page 65

Eggs Goldenrod, page 64

Buffalo Potato Wedges, page 35

Peppermint Punch, page 10

Martha Washingtons, page 170

Hamburger Noodle Casserole, page 36

Cheesecake Cranberry Bars, page 160

Cheesy Spinach & Sausage Bake, page 39

Cheddar Potato Gratin, page 99

Emma's Gingerbread Muffins, page 48

Tomato-Ravioli Soup, page 72

Mac & Cheese Nuggets, page 40

Pineapple-Cranberry Pork Roast, page 115

Fluffy French Bread Stuffing, page 114

Pecan Cookie Balls, page 156

German Apple Streusel Kuchen, page 134

Festive *Christmas* Dinner

Tuscan Chicken & Olives

Denise Mainville
Huber Heights, OH

This savory chicken is especially good served over cooked fresh spinach.

2 to 2-1/2 lbs. boneless,
   skinless chicken breasts
2 T. olive oil
1-1/4 t. pesto seasoning

1/2 c. Kalamata olives, pitted
1/2 c. white wine or chicken
   broth

In a large skillet over medium heat, cook chicken in oil for 15 minutes, turning to brown evenly. Drain; reduce heat. Sprinkle seasoning evenly over chicken. Add olives; drizzle with wine or broth. Cover tightly and simmer for 25 minutes. Uncover; continue cooking for 5 to 10 minutes, until chicken is no longer pink. Serves 4.

Turn old Christmas cards and leftover giftwrap into placemats!
Protect your creations by sandwiching placemats between
two sheets of clear self-adhesive plastic...they'll perk up
the dinner table throughout the season.

Susana's Shrimp Rigatoni

Susana Dejesa
Hagatna, Guam

*We enjoyed this dish at a popular Italian restaurant on our island.
I just had to try and replicate the recipe...here's the yummy result!*

1/2 lb. spinach
1/2 c. butter
1 pt. whipping cream
1/8 t. garlic powder
1/8 t. pepper
1/4 c. shredded Parmesan
  cheese

salt to taste
1 lb. uncooked large shrimp,
  peeled
12-oz. pkg. rigatoni pasta,
  cooked
1 c. shredded mozzarella cheese

Blanch spinach in boiling water. Drain; press out excess water and set
aside. Melt butter in a large saucepan over medium heat. Add cream,
garlic powder and pepper; bring to a slow boil. Reduce heat and
simmer for 10 minutes, stirring frequently. Add Parmesan cheese; stir
until melted. Add salt to taste; remove pan from heat after 2 minutes.
Stir shrimp into cream sauce. Spread cooked pasta evenly in a lightly
greased 13"x9" baking pan; top with spinach. Pour cream sauce with
shrimp over pasta and spinach. Mix all together, coating well with
sauce; spread out mixture evenly in pan. Spread mozzarella cheese
over top. Bake, uncovered, at 375 degrees until cheese is golden and
melted, about 30 minutes. Makes 6 servings.

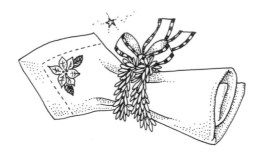

Make mini wreaths of pine-scented rosemary to slip around
dinner napkins. Simply wind fresh rosemary stems into a
ring shape, tuck in the ends and tie on a tiny bow...so festive!

Festive Holiday Gingerbread

Peggy Anderson
Easton, CT

When I lived in rural England. I baked this delicious dessert for a charity cake stall at a village fair. It was the top bid of all the cakes on offer, and the following year, buyers were clamoring for it again! I made many new friends in the village by baking it often.

12-oz. jar light molasses
1 c. butter, softened
3/4 c. dark brown sugar, packed
2 eggs, beaten
1 c. hot water
4 c. all-purpose flour
2 t. baking soda
1/2 t. salt
2-1/2 t. ground ginger
1/2 t. cinnamon
9-oz. pkg. condensed
mincemeat, finely crumbled
Garnish: powdered sugar

In a large bowl, combine all ingredients except mincemeat and powdered sugar. Beat with an electric mixer on medium speed for 2 to 3 minutes, until well blended. Fold in mincemeat; spoon into a greased large Bundt® or tube pan. Bake at 350 degrees for 45 to 50 minutes. Cool for 10 minutes. Turn out onto a wire rack to cool completely. Dust with powdered sugar. Makes 10 to 12 servings.

Baby photos make the sweetest placecards...just copy, cut out and place in mini frames.

Holiday *Open House*

Butter Pecan Bundt Cake

LeAnn Keener
Rush Center, KS

*This cake is so easy and so moist...it doesn't even need to be
frosted because there's frosting baked right in!*

18-oz. pkg. butter pecan
   cake mix
15-oz. can coconut-pecan
   frosting
3 eggs, beaten

3/4 c. oil
1 c. water
1/2 c. chopped pecans
Garnish: vanilla ice cream

Combine all ingredients except ice cream in a large bowl. Stir to blend;
beat for 2 minutes with an electric mixer on high speed. Pour into a
greased and floured Bundt® pan. Bake at 350 degrees for 55 minutes,
or until cake is firm. Cool for 15 minutes before inverting onto a
serving plate. Serve slices topped with scoops of ice cream. Makes
10 to 12 servings.

Choose a theme for holiday decorating...Silver Bells, Farmhouse
Kitchen, A White Christmas are a few ideas. Then carry out your
theme throughout the house...Christmas tree ornaments,
the front door wreath, the garland on the mantel and
even a dinner table centerpiece. Clever!

German Apple Streusel Kuchen

Karin Anderson
Hillsboro, OH

I was born and raised in Germany, so naturally I am always looking for recipes reminding me of my childhood. Baking this cake brings back so many beautiful memories of my parents and brothers.

1 loaf frozen bread dough, thawed
4 Granny Smith apples, cored, peeled and thinly sliced
3/4 c. plus 1/3 c. sugar, divided
1 t. cinnamon
1 T. vanilla extract
1/4 c. sliced almonds
1/4 c. butter, melted
1-1/4 c. all-purpose flour

Let dough rise according to package directions. Spread out dough on a greased 16"x11" baking sheet. Let rise again for 20 to 25 minutes. Mix apples, 3/4 cup sugar, cinnamon and vanilla; spread apple mixture evenly over dough. Sprinkle with almonds; set aside. In a small bowl, combine butter, flour and remaining sugar; mix with fingertips or a fork until crumbly. Spread evenly over apple layer. Bake at 375 degrees for 25 minutes. Cut into squares to serve. Makes 24 servings.

Twist together fluffy red & white pipe cleaners into "candy canes" in a jiffy! Quick & easy...tie onto gifts from your kitchen or evergreen wreaths.

Holiday *Open House*

Date-Nut Cake

Debbie Jarrell
Roanoke, VA

This recipe was from my Grandmother who came to the US from England in the late 1800's as a child. I remember it being served by my aunt every Christmas.

2 c. chopped dates
2 t. baking soda
2 c. boiling water
2 T. butter, softened
2 eggs, beaten

2 t. vanilla extract
2 c. sugar
1/8 t. salt
3 c. all-purpose flour
1 c. walnuts or pecans, chopped

Place dates in a large bowl and sprinkle with baking soda; pour boiling water over dates. Let cool. Add remaining ingredients and mix well. Pour into a greased Bundt® pan. Bake at 350 degrees for about 50 minutes. Makes 10 to 12 servings.

Turn a Bundt® cake into a holiday wreath. Drizzle with frosting, then sprinkle chopped green and red candied cherries over the top. Twist a long strip of red fruit leather into a jaunty bow to complete the wreath...simple!

Kick-the-Can Ice Cream

Beth Bundy
Long Prairie, MN

My kids love to make this every Christmas...it's such fun and helps them work off a little of their extra school vacation energy.

1 pasteurized egg, beaten
1 c. milk
1 c. half-and-half
1/2 c. sugar
3.4-oz. pkg. instant vanilla
   pudding mix

3/4 t. vanilla extract
1/8 t. salt
crushed ice
2 T. rock salt

Mix all ingredients together. Pour into a one-pound coffee can or other small container. Use duct tape to seal lid tightly. Place small coffee can into a 3-pound coffee can. Pack crushed ice around it; sprinkle ice with coarse salt. Seal lid tightly onto larger can. Take can outside on a cold day and gently kick or roll can for 15 minutes or longer. If ice cream isn't quite set, place in freezer and shake occasionally until set. Makes 3 cups.

Simply Sweet

Renee Suits
McCalla, AL

My husband's grandfather just loved this dessert. He would always ask me if I was going to fix it for a holiday meal. We caught him one year hiding small amounts around the kitchen!

16-oz. container frozen whipped
   topping, thawed
6-oz. pkg. favorite-flavor
   gelatin mix

15-oz. can fruit cocktail, drained
1-1/2 c. chopped nuts, divided

Combine whipped topping and gelatin in a large bowl; add fruit. Stir in one cup nuts; mix until well blended. Sprinkle with remaining nuts; refrigerate until ready to serve. Makes 6 to 8 servings.

Holiday *Open House*

Christmas Chocolate Roll

Sue Rosa
New Bern, NC

Grandma Batchelor always had a big family gathering at Christmastime with lots of home-baked goodies. Her chocolate roll was a special favorite that still brings back some of my best childhood memories. These are so easy to make that I usually make 6 to 12 rolls to give as gifts!

1 c. cake flour	4 eggs
1 t. baking powder	1 c. sugar
1/4 t. salt	1/2 t. vanilla extract
2 T. margarine, melted	Optional: powdered sugar
1/3 c. hot water	

Sift together cake flour, baking powder and salt; set aside. Combine margarine and hot water in a cup; let cool slightly. Beat eggs in a separate large bowl, gradually adding sugar and vanilla. Add margarine mixture to egg mixture, beating slowly. Slowly add flour mixture until smooth; batter will be very thin. Pour evenly into a wax paper-lined 15"x10" jelly-roll pan. Bake at 400 degrees for about 15 minutes, until lightly golden. Invert hot cake onto a tea towel. Peel off wax paper; trim edges all around cake. Roll cake up in tea towel and let cool. Unroll cake. Spread Chocolate Syrup over cake, adding as much or as little as desired. Allow syrup to soak into the cake; roll cake into a log. Sprinkle with powdered sugar, if desired. Makes 12 to 15 servings.

Chocolate Syrup:

1-1/2 c. sugar	1/2 c. water
7 to 8 T. baking cocoa	

Heat ingredients to a boil, stirring constantly. Cool slightly.

Marshmallow Pudding

Kathleen Walker
Mountain Center, CA

My great-grandmother would spend Saturday afternoons canning preserves or baking pies. Marshmallow Pudding was one of her favorite desserts to make when I visited. I can still remember sitting in her cozy living room, listening to her cuckoo clock and smelling the aroma coming from her kitchen...a place where EVERYTHING was made from scratch.

5 c. mini marshmallows
1/3 c. milk
1 pt. whipping cream
1/3 c. cranberry juice cocktail

.3-oz. sugar-free strawberry
   gelatin mix
1/4 c. powdered sugar
1/4 c. chopped pecans

Place marshmallows and milk in the top of a double boiler over hot water. Cook over medium heat until marshmallows melt. Remove from heat; stir well and let cool. In a separate bowl, beat whipping cream with an electric mixer on high speed until stiff peaks form. Fold whipped cream into marshmallow mixture; set aside. Heat cranberry juice until very hot; stir in gelatin until dissolved. Cool until beginning to set, about 2 hours. Whip until well mixed; add to marshmallow mixture. Mix in powdered sugar and nuts. Spoon into an ungreased 13"x9" baking pan. Chill thoroughly before serving. Makes 8 to 10 servings.

A red sugar bucket looks cheerful filled with green Granny Smith apples. Set it by the kitchen door for a holiday welcome.

Holiday *Open House*

Chocolate Fondue

Echo Renner
Meeteetse, WY

My Aunt Karen made this fondue every year on Christmas Eve and New Year's Eve. Our extended family would gather around the fondue pot enjoying this delectable treat...yum!

2 8-oz. chocolate candy bars, plain or with almonds
2 to 4 T. light cream
Optional: 1 t. cherry brandy or peppermint liqueur

marshmallows
banana and pineapple chunks
maraschino cherries
pound cake, cubed
shortbread cookies

Break chocolate bars into pieces; place in an electric fondue pot. Heat on low setting until chocolate is melted, stirring in cream to desired thickness. Add liqueur to taste, if using; stir until smooth. Serve with desired items for dipping into warm chocolate with fondue forks. Makes 8 to 10 servings.

Serve up a snowy dessert buffet. Arrange inverted cake pans or bowls on a table to create different levels, then cover with cottony white batting. Sprinkle with sparkling silver glitter and set desserts on top...magical!

Spumoni Cake

Ann Maddix
Pawtucket, RI

*We always knew Christmas was coming when Mom began
to bake her special Spumoni Cake!*

18-1/4 oz. pkg. yellow cake mix
8-oz. container sour cream
3.4-oz. pkg. instant vanilla
 pudding mix
1/2 c. chopped nuts
2 t. almond extract, divided
6 drops green food coloring

8-oz. jar red maraschino
 cherries, drained and
 chopped
6 drops red food coloring
3 T. baking cocoa
Garnish: powdered sugar

Prepare cake mix according to package directions. Stir in sour cream and dry pudding mix; divide batter into 3 bowls. To first bowl, add nuts, one teaspoon almond extract and green coloring. To second bowl, add cherries, remaining extract and red coloring. To third bowl, add cocoa. In same order, without mixing, pour batters into a greased and floured Bundt® pan. Bake at 350 degrees for 50 to 60 minutes. Sprinkle cooled cake with powdered sugar. Serves 10 to 12.

Sparkly sanding sugar gives frosted cakes and cookies a pretty snow-dusted look. Sprinkle on while the frosting is still wet, wait 5 minutes, then gently shake off any excess.

Holiday *Open House*

Red Velvet Cake

Angela Miller
Jefferson City, MO

*My grandma and aunt make this wonderful cake for my birthday
in November and I usually make it again for Christmas. The
homemade frosting is scrumptious...well worth the time!*

18-1/4 oz. pkg. fudge marble
   cake mix
1 t. baking soda
2 eggs, beaten

1-1/2 c. buttermilk
1-oz. bottle red food coloring
1 t. vanilla extract

Combine dry cake mix and baking soda in a medium bowl; add
remaining ingredients. Blend with an electric mixer on low speed
until moistened. Beat on high speed for 2 minutes. Pour batter into
2 greased and floured 9" round cake pans. Bake at 350 degrees for
30 to 35 minutes, until cake tests done. Cool in pans for 10 minutes;
turn out onto a wire rack. Cool completely; if desired, freeze layers
overnight to make cake easier to frost. Frost between layers, top and
sides of cake. If frozen, thaw one hour before serving. Makes 10 to
12 servings.

Vanilla Frosting:

5 T. all-purpose flour
1 c. milk
1 c. butter, softened

1 c. sugar
2 t. vanilla extract

Whisk flour and milk in a saucepan over medium-low heat until
smooth. Bring to a boil; cook and stir for 2 minutes, or until
thickened. Cover and refrigerate. In a medium bowl, blend butter
and sugar; add chilled milk mixture. Beat for 10 minutes, or until
fluffy. Stir in vanilla.

Vivian's Prune Cake

Debbie Mullis
Concord, NC

My mom has made this cake for over 50 years. It is a very moist spicy cake with chocolate icing...and you know, everything tastes better with chocolate! She would bake a cake on Saturday and it would not be cut until Sunday and as long as it lasted, you enjoyed cake all week.

16-oz. pkg. dried pitted plums
4 eggs
2 c. sugar
1/4 c. butter, softened
2 c. all-purpose flour

2 t. baking soda
1/8 t. salt
1 t. cinnamon
1 t. ground cloves
1 t. nutmeg

Cover dried plums with water in a medium saucepan. Simmer over low heat until soft, about 30 minutes. Drain plums, reserving one cup liquid; mash with a potato masher and set aside. With an electric mixer on medium speed, beat eggs and sugar together; mix in butter, plums and reserved liquid. Add flour, baking soda, salt and spices; mix well. Pour batter into 3 greased and floured 9" round cake pans. Bake at 350 degrees for 20 to 30 minutes. Cool; assemble with Chocolate Icing. Serves 10 to 12.

Chocolate Icing:

1/2 c. butter
1/4 c. baking cocoa
1 t. vanilla extract

16-oz. pkg. powdered sugar
Optional: 1 to 3 T. evaporated
milk

Melt butter in a saucepan over low heat; add cocoa and vanilla. Stir in powdered sugar. If too thick, add milk to right consistency.

Holiday *Open House*

Raisin Pie

Linda Richard
Carmel, ME

*My French-Canadian grandmother baked this pie for my aunts' &
uncles' co-workers...almost daily! I never knew her, but while I was
working on my genealogy, I was thrilled to find out that this was one of
her specialties. I still have her wooden rolling pin too, handed down to
me from my mother.*

2 c. water	1/8 t. salt
2 c. raisins	butter to taste
1/2 c. brown sugar, packed	2 t. vanilla extract
1/4 c. sugar	1 t. lemon juice
2 T. cornstarch	2 refrigerated pie crusts

Bring water to boil in a saucepan over medium heat; add raisins.
Reduce heat and simmer for 5 minutes, until raisins are plump.
Combine sugars, cornstarch and salt in a large bowl; stir into raisins.
Cook over low heat, stirring constantly, until mixture boils and
thickens, about 3 minutes. Stir in butter, vanilla and lemon juice;
remove from heat. Arrange one crust in a 9" pie plate. Pour filling
into unbaked crust. Cover with top crust; seal and vent crust. Bake
at 425 degrees for 20 minutes, or until golden. Serves 6 to 8.

Bring old-fashioned charm to your kitchen. Use strands
of raffia to tie sprigs of boxwood to vintage cookie jars,
antique sifters, apothecary jars and milk bottles.

Sticky Toffee Puddings

Denise Neal
Castle Rock, CO

My husband and I first tried this dessert in a quaint village pub while on vacation in England. I just had to have the recipe so I could make it at home! I love the gooey sauce...sometimes I even double the toffee coating mixture to have more yummy topping with my dessert!

4 T. butter, softened
3/4 c. sugar
1 egg, beaten
1 c. all-purpose flour
1 t. baking powder

3/4 c. chopped dates
1-1/4 c. boiling water
1 t. baking soda
1 t. vanilla extract
Garnish: whipped cream

Blend butter and sugar well; stir in egg and set aside. Sift together flour and baking powder. Add gradually to butter mixture; mix well. Place dates in a bowl and pour boiling water over top; add baking soda and vanilla. Mix well and add to butter mixture. Pour into 6 greased 5" mini pie plates. Bake at 350 degrees for 30 minutes, or until puddings test done with a toothpick. Spoon Toffee Coating over hot puddings; place under broiler just until coating begins to bubble (careful, it burns easily!). Serve warm, topped with a dollop of whipped cream. Makes 6 servings.

Toffee Coating:

1/3 c. brown sugar, packed
2 T. butter, softened

2 T. whipping cream

Beat together all ingredients. Simmer in a small saucepan for about 3 minutes, until brown sugar dissolves.

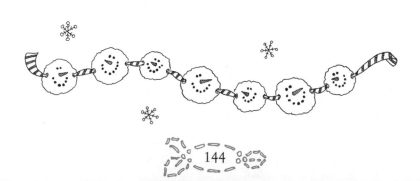

Holiday *Open House*

Boiled Custard

Sonya McKenzie
Clarksville, TN

I always looked forward to my grandmother Mary Ruth's sweet, rich boiled custard as much as Christmas and Santa Claus himself... after 40 years, she finally passed the recipe along to me!

2 c. sugar
6 T. all-purpose flour
8 egg yolks, beaten

1-1/2 qts. whole milk
1 T. vanilla extract
Optional: nutmeg

Mix sugar and flour together; add egg yolks, milk and vanilla. Whisk well; strain mixture to remove any lumps. Pour into a large heavy saucepan over medium-low heat. Cook for about 30 minutes, or until mixture coats a wooden spoon, stirring constantly to prevent sticking. Cool for 30 minutes; spoon into a 2-quart container and chill overnight. Spoon into serving glasses; sprinkle with nutmeg, if desired. Makes 12 servings.

Make some sweet & simple button wreaths. Choose buttons from Grandma's button box or pick up a supply at a craft store. Simply thread large, flat buttons onto wire, then twist the ends to form a circle. Tie on a fluffy bow and they're ready to embellish a gift from your kitchen!

Grandpa Jim's Cake

Sheila Gwaltney
Johnson City, TN

Unbelievably scrumptious!

18-1/4 oz. pkg. German
    chocolate cake mix
14-oz. can sweetened
    condensed milk
3/4 c. butterscotch ice cream
    topping

8-oz. container frozen whipped
    topping, thawed
2 1.4-oz. chocolate-covered
    toffee bars, crushed

Prepare cake as directed on package; bake in a 13"x9" baking pan.
Poke holes in cake while still warm; pour condensed milk and ice
cream topping over cake. Cool. Frost with whipped topping; top with
crushed candy. Keep refrigerated. Makes 12 to 16 servings.

Rum Cake

Deana Osborne
Somerset, KY

My great-uncle's recipe...the best and easiest rum cake ever!

18-1/4 oz. pkg. golden butter
    cake mix
4 eggs, beaten

1/2 c. oil
1/2 c. water
1/2 c. light rum

Beat all ingredients together for 2 minutes. Pour into a greased and
floured Bundt® pan. Bake at 325 degrees for 50 to 60 minutes.
Remove cake from pan immediately; pour Rum Sauce over warm
cake. Serves 8 to 12.

Rum Sauce:

1 c. sugar
1/2 c. butter

1/4 c. water
1/4 c. light rum

In a small saucepan, cook ingredients together for 3 to 5 minutes.

Holiday *Open House*

Upside-Down Apple Spice Cake

Shirley Bowles
Wyoming, DE

Every year as the leaves begin to turn and the air cools down, I think of this recipe. I am 72 and for as long as I can remember, my mother made this at least once a month. Now I carry on the tradition, using a tattered recipe card from the 1950's.

1/4 c. plus 3 T. shortening, divided
1/2 t. cinnamon
1/4 t. nutmeg
1/4 t. allspice
1/2 t. salt
3/4 c. sugar
1 egg, beaten

1-1/4 c. all-purpose flour
1-1/2 t. baking powder
1/2 c. plus 2 T. milk, divided
2 c. apples, cored, peeled and sliced
1 T. butter
1/2 c. brown sugar, packed

Combine 1/4 cup shortening, spices and salt in a large bowl. Add sugar gradually; blend until light and fluffy. Add egg; beat thoroughly. Mix flour and baking powder together. Add small amounts of flour to shortening mixture alternately with 1/2 cup milk, beating after each addition until smooth. Set batter aside. Arrange apple slices in a greased 8"x8" baking pan. Melt butter and remaining shortening together; add brown sugar and remaining milk. Mix well and spread over apples; pour batter carefully over all. Bake at 350 degrees for 50 to 60 minutes. Immediately invert pan onto a serving plate or tray. Let stand for 5 minutes before removing pan. Makes 8 to 10 servings.

Ring in the holidays! Tie a jingle bell or two onto napkin rings or around Mason jars filled with Christmas candy.

Punch Bowl Cake

Suzanne Varnes
Palatka, FL

*A cool, creamy fruit dessert that's quick & easy to make, yet looks
like you went to a lot of effort! It even freezes well...just thaw
in the fridge before serving time.*

16-oz. container frozen whipped
  topping, thawed
14-oz. can sweetened
  condensed milk
8-oz. pkg. cream cheese,
  softened
1 t. vanilla extract

1 angel food cake, cubed
21-oz. can blueberry, peach,
  cherry or strawberry pie
  filling
Optional: fresh fruit slices,
  fresh mint sprigs

In a large bowl, combine whipped topping, condensed milk, cream
cheese and vanilla. Beat until creamy; set aside. In a large clear glass
bowl, place a layer of cake cubes, a layer of pie filling and a layer of
topping mixture. Be generous with cake and topping mixture, but just
drizzle pie filling around edges and over center. Repeat layers. Cover
with plastic wrap and refrigerate overnight before serving. Garnish
with fresh fruit or mint, if desired. Serves 10 to 12.

Sugared berries are a sparkling garnish for desserts.
Brush whole raspberries or blueberries with
corn syrup, then roll in coarse sugar.

Holiday *Open House*

Great-Aunt Stella's Gob Cake

Renee Yates
Falls Church, VA

You know you're in for a treat when you go to Pennsylvania and taste this wonderful chocolate cake, sandwiched with creamy white filling.

18-1/2 oz. chocolate cake mix
3.9-oz. pkg. instant chocolate
   pudding mix
2-1/2 c. milk, divided
1/3 c. oil
3.4-oz. pkg. instant vanilla
   pudding mix

1/2 c. shortening
1/2 c. margarine, softened
1 c. powdered sugar
1 t. vanilla extract
Optional: additional powdered
   sugar

Combine cake mix, chocolate pudding mix, 1-1/2 cups milk and oil. Beat with an electric mixer on high speed for 4 minutes. Spread in 2 greased and floured 9" round cake pans. Bake at 350 degrees for 20 to 25 minutes. Cool layers on a wire rack. For filling, prepare vanilla pudding mix with remaining milk; chill until very cold. Blend shortening and margarine; add chilled pudding, powdered sugar and vanilla. Beat with an electric mixer on high speed for 10 minutes. Place one layer on a plate; spread with filling. Add second layer on top; sprinkle with powdered sugar, if desired. Makes 10 to 12 servings.

A forest of tiny trees! Decorate sugar cones with green icing and arrange on a platter of sparkly white sanding sugar.

GiGi's Cranberry Cobbler

Dawn Horton
Allen, TX

We all look forward to this cobbler each Christmas when my sweet mother-in-law makes it. Be sure to buy the fresh cranberries ahead of time, though...one year, we spent several hours with the whole family in the van driving from store to store hunting for cranberries!

3 c. biscuit baking mix
2 c. sugar
2 eggs, beaten

1/2 c. butter, softened
1 c. milk
3 c. cranberries

Mix baking mix, sugar, eggs and butter together; blend in milk. Stir in cranberries lightly, until evenly coated with batter. Pour into a greased and floured 13"x9" baking pan. Bake at 350 degrees for 50 to 55 minutes. Spoon Hot Butter Sauce over warm cobbler. Serves 8 to 10.

Hot Butter Sauce:

2 c. sugar
1 c. butter

2 c. whipping cream
2 t. vanilla extract

Mix ingredients together in a deep saucepan over medium heat. Bring to a boil. Boil for about 5 minutes, stirring constantly.

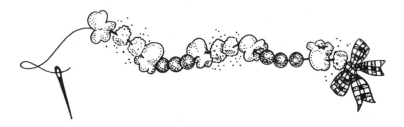

Waxed dental floss is super for stringing old-fashioned garlands of cranberries and popcorn. It's stronger than regular thread and the waxed coating slides right through...what a super tip!

Holiday *Open House*

Apple-Cranberry Pie

Susan Bick
Ballwin, MO

Serve slices of this delightful pie at your next holiday open house.

2 9-inch pie crusts	2 c. cranberries
1-3/4 c. sugar	2 T. butter, diced
1/4 c. all-purpose flour	
3 c. tart apples, cored, peeled and sliced	

Line a 9" pie plate with one crust; set aside. Mix sugar and flour together. Alternate layers of apples, cranberries and sugar mixture in crust. Dot with butter; cover with remaining crust. Seal crusts together and cut small slits in top. Bake at 425 degrees for 40 to 50 minutes, or until crust is golden and juice begins to bubble through slits in crust. Makes 6 to 8 servings.

N is for Nuts with a Nutcracker handy.
O is for Oranges and Oodles of candy.
P is Plum Puddings with hard sauce on top,
and Pies made of Pumpkin, and Popcorn to Pop.
– Marion Conger

Egg Custard Pie

Hope Davenport
Portland, TX

An old-time favorite...dollop with freshly whipped cream.

6 eggs, beaten
1 c. sugar
1 t. vanilla extract
1/2 t. salt

2-1/2 c. milk
9-inch pie crust
1/2 t. nutmeg

Beat together eggs, sugar, vanilla, salt and milk, mixing well. Strain to remove any lumps. Pour into pie crust; sprinkle with nutmeg. Bake at 450 degrees for 10 minutes. Decrease oven temperature to 350 degrees; bake for an additional 45 minutes. Serves 6 to 8.

Start a tradition of filling stockings with old-fashioned small gifts like penny candy, wooden puzzles, tiny toys and a juicy piece of ripe fruit. You may be surprised at how eagerly these surprises will be anticipated!

Cookies
by the Dozen

Grandma Gray's Spice-Nut Bars

Kelly Wood
Salem, OH

This recipe belonged to my great-grandmother on my mother's side. Mother made these cookie bars every Christmas and the aromatic spices of cinnamon, nutmeg and cloves remind me of the holidays...they are always gobbled up immediately!

1-1/2 c. all-purpose flour
1/2 t. baking powder
1/2 t. baking soda
1/2 t. salt
1/2 t. cinnamon
1/4 t. nutmeg
1/8 t. ground cloves
1/4 c. margarine, softened

1 c. brown sugar, packed
1 egg, beaten
1/2 c. plus 1 T. hot coffee,
   divided
1/2 c. raisins
1/2 c. chopped walnuts
1/2 c. powdered sugar

In a medium bowl, combine flour, baking powder, baking soda, salt and spices; set aside. In a large bowl, blend together margarine, brown sugar and egg. Add 1/2 cup coffee; stir in raisins and walnuts. Stir in flour mixture. Pour into a greased 13"x9" baking pan. Bake at 350 degrees for 15 to 20 minutes, or until lightly golden on top. Remove from oven; immediately prepare glaze by combining powdered sugar with remaining coffee. Spread glaze over bars; cut into bars while still warm. Makes about 2 dozen.

Wrap up some home-baked treats to send to a service person overseas...they're sure to be appreciated. Tuck in a note that says, "We're thinking of you." The American Red Cross can provide information on how to mail care packages.

Cookies by the Dozen

Vanilla Men

Shelley La Due
Victoria, Australia

A fun change from the gingerbread boys we all grew up with!

1-3/4 c. self-rising flour, divided
1/8 t. salt
1/3 c. sugar
1 egg, beaten
1 t. vanilla extract

6 T. butter, melted
1/4 to 1/2 c. milk
Garnish: currants, candied
   cherries

Sift together one cup flour and salt; set aside. Blend sugar, egg and vanilla; add flour mixture and stir well. Add melted butter; beat well. Stir in remaining flour and mix to a firm dough; wrap and chill well. Roll out thinly on a lightly floured surface; cut out cookies with a gingerbread man cutter. Place on greased baking sheets; brush cookies with milk. Decorate, adding currants for eyes, nose and buttons, and a cherry slice for mouth. Bake at 350 degrees for 15 to 20 minutes, or until firm and golden. Makes about 15.

Festoon a doorway or mantel with a garland of gingerbread people. After cutting out cookie dough, make a small hole in each "hand" with a drinking straw. Bake and decorate cookies, then tie them together side-by-side with narrow ribbon threaded through the holes.

Pecan Cookie Balls

Jodi Eisenhooth
McVeytown, PA

*Make these sweet, crisp little morsels to go with an
after-dinner cup of tea or coffee.*

1 c. butter, softened
1 c. powdered sugar
2 c. chopped pecans

1 T. vanilla extract
2 c. all-purpose flour
4 T. powdered sugar

Blend together butter and powdered sugar; add pecans, vanilla and
flour. Wrap dough in plastic wrap; chill for about 3 hours. Form
dough into 3/4-inch balls; place on ungreased baking sheets. Bake at
350 degrees for 10 minutes. Let cool; roll in powdered sugar. Makes
2-1/2 to 3 dozen.

Grandma's Butter Cookies

Sue Dangler
Cecil, OH

*My father was a salesman when I was growing up. After an
especially good month, my mother could afford to buy butter
to make his favorite butter cookies...such a treat!*

1 lb. butter, softened
1 c. cornstarch

1 c. powdered sugar
2 c. all-purpose flour

Blend all ingredients together; divide into 2 logs. Wrap in wax paper;
refrigerate overnight. Slice logs 1/2-inch thick; cut each slice into
quarters. Arrange on ungreased baking sheets. Bake at 325 degrees
for 18 to 20 minutes. Cool on paper towels. Makes 3 to 4 dozen.

Cookies by the Dozen

Mama's Tea Cakes

Robin Herrin
South Valdosta, GA

My mama and I spent such precious times baking together. I can almost smell the sweet, rich aroma of her tea cakes now! I miss my wonderful mama so much...she was well-known for her good cooking and thankfully she passed it down to me.

1/2 c. margarine, softened
1 c. sugar
1 egg, beaten
1/2 t. vanilla extract

2-3/4 c. self-rising flour, sifted
2 to 3 T. milk
Optional: egg white, colored
    sugar

Blend margarine and sugar until fluffy. Add egg and vanilla; mix well. Add flour to mixture; stir in milk, one teaspoon at a time, until a soft dough forms. Roll out on a floured surface; cut into desired shapes. Place on lightly greased baking sheets. If desired, brush with beaten egg white and sprinkle tops with colored sugar. Bake at 350 degrees for 8 to 10 minutes. Store in an airtight container. Makes about 3 dozen.

For a gift that will be welcomed by a busy friend, pack a dozen cookies along with a soothing tea blend. Mix one cup each of organic chamomile and lavender flowers from a health food store. Place in a decorative jar and tie on a tea infuser. So thoughtful!

Mom's Fail-Proof Fudge

Stefanie Schmidt
Las Vegas, NV

Growing up, I always knew Christmas was on the way,
once my mom and I had made the chocolate fudge!

3 c. sugar
3/4 c. margarine
2/3 c. evaporated milk
12-oz. pkg. semi-sweet
    chocolate chips

7-oz. jar marshmallow creme
1 t. vanilla extract
1 c. chopped walnuts

Combine sugar, margarine and evaporated milk in a large heavy
saucepan. Bring to a full rolling boil over medium heat, stirring
constantly. Continue boiling for 5 minutes over medium heat, stirring
constantly. Remove from heat; stir in chocolate chips until melted.
Add marshmallow creme, vanilla and nuts; beat until well blended.
Pour into a greased 13"x9" baking pan. Cool at room temperature;
cut into bite-size squares. Makes about 3 pounds.

Mocha fudge is a coffee lover's delight. Simply stir in a
heaping tablespoon of instant coffee granules along
with the sugar. Heap individually wrapped squares
in a brand new coffee mug...clever!

Cookies by the Dozen

Creamy Pecan Pralines

Martha Coody
Pascagoula, MS

My mom made this delicious candy every Christmas to give as gifts. She would stand at the stove stirring until the candy was just right. I got to help wrap the pieces in wax paper and place them in cookie tins she'd saved. I will never forget the great times we had in the kitchen, cooking and sharing.

1-1/2 c. sugar	1/8 t. baking soda
3/4 c. brown sugar, packed	1 T. margarine
1 c. milk	1 t. vanilla extract
1/8 t. salt	1 c. chopped pecans

Mix sugars, milk and salt in a large heavy saucepan. Bring to a boil over medium heat; add baking soda and margarine. Cook until mixture reaches the firm-ball stage, or 244 to 249 degrees on a candy thermometer. Remove from heat; add vanilla and pecans. Stir until sugary. Drop onto wax paper by tablespoonfuls. If candy becomes too hard to drop, add a teaspoon of milk to thin. Wrap pralines in squares of wax paper. Makes 12 to 14.

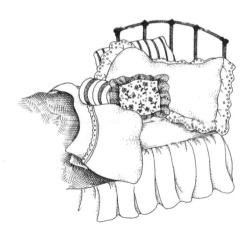

The children were nestled all snug in their beds
While visions of sugarplums danced in their heads.
– Clement Moore

Cheesecake Cranberry Bars

Linda Galvin
Ames, IA

A friend of mine served these creamy, tangy dessert bars when she hosted a holiday tea...I just had to have the recipe!

2 c. all-purpose flour
1-1/2 c. long-cooking oats, uncooked
1/4 c. brown sugar, packed
1 c. butter, softened
12-oz. pkg. white chocolate chips
8-oz. pkg. cream cheese, softened

14-oz. can sweetened condensed milk
1/4 c. lemon juice
1 t. vanilla extract
16-oz. can whole-berry cranberry sauce
2 T. cornstarch

Combine flour, oats and brown sugar in a large bowl. Add butter; mix until crumbly. Stir in chocolate chips; reserve 2-1/2 cups of crumb mixture for topping. With floured fingers, press remaining mixture into a greased 13"x9" baking pan; set aside. Beat cream cheese in a large bowl until creamy. Add condensed milk, lemon juice and vanilla. Mix until smooth and pour over crust. Combine cranberry sauce and cornstarch; spoon over cream cheese mixture. Sprinkle reserved crumb mixture over top. Bake at 375 degrees for 35 to 40 minutes, or until golden. Cool; cut into bars. Makes 2 dozen.

Place Cheesecake Cranberry Bars in paper muffin liners and set on a platter...oh-so easy for everyone to serve themselves at a dessert party.

Cookies by the Dozen

Pink & Green Date Cookies

Jennifer Martineau
Delaware, OH

This recipe is from my Great-Grandmother Dietz...when I got married, my sister passed it along to me in a recipe box of family favorites.

1 c. butter
2 c. brown sugar, packed
2 eggs, beaten
2 8-oz. pkgs. dates, very finely chopped
1 c. chopped pecans

4 c. all-purpose flour
1 t. baking powder
1 t. baking soda
1/2 t. salt
1/4 c. cold water

Blend butter and brown sugar in a large bowl. Add eggs, mixing in by hand; stir in dates and pecans. In a separate bowl, mix flour, baking powder, baking soda and salt. Add flour mixture to butter mixture alternately with water; mix well. Form into rolls, about one inch in diameter. Wrap rolls in wax paper and freeze. Slice frozen dough 1/4-inch thick with a serrated knife. Arrange on ungreased baking sheets. Bake at 280 degrees for 7 minutes; do not overbake. If cookies are difficult to remove from baking sheets, let stand for a few minutes. Ice with glaze while still warm. Makes 20 to 25 dozen.

Glaze:

6 T. butter, melted and cooled
6 T. milk
5-1/2 c. powdered sugar

few drops green and red food coloring

Mix butter and milk; stir in powdered sugar until thick. Divide into 2 bowls; tint one bowl green and the other bowl pink with food coloring.

Cream Cheese Candy

Bonnie Weatherford
Aurora, IN

*This was my dad's favorite Christmas candy...just one taste
brings back memories of a really great dad & grandpa!*

8-oz. pkg. cream cheese,
  softened
1 c. milk

2 lbs. powdered sugar
3/4 to 1 c. creamy peanut butter

Mix cream cheese and powdered sugar; divide into 4 balls. Roll each
ball out 1/4-inch thick on wax paper to form a rectangle. Spread
peanut butter on top. Roll up from long end and slice 1/2-inch thick.
Chill slightly. Store between wax paper in a covered container. Makes
4 dozen.

Peanut Butter Drops

Faith Harris
Orlinda, TN

*My mother used to make this fudge for the 10 of us kids when we were
growing up. Our family didn't have a lot of money, so it was perfect for
us. My mother is now 90 years old and I think of her when I make this
fudge. My daughter won first place with this recipe when she entered it
in the county fair for her 4-H project.*

1/2 c. creamy or crunchy peanut
  butter
1 c. milk

2 c. sugar
1 t. vanilla extract

Combine peanut butter, milk and sugar in a large heavy saucepan
over medium heat. Cook until mixture reaches the soft-ball stage, or
234 to 243 degrees on a candy thermometer. Add vanilla; beat with
an electric mixer on low speed until fudge begins to lose its gloss.
Immediately drop onto wax paper by tablespoonfuls. Let stand at
room temperature until set. Makes about 1-1/2 dozen.

Cookies by the Dozen

Twice-Cooked Divinity

*Patty Fosnight
Childress, TX*

*This is a childhood favorite of mine...Grandmother
would make this for every holiday.*

2 c. sugar
1/3 c. water
1/8 t. salt

1/2 c. corn syrup, divided
2 egg whites, stiffly beaten
Optional: 1/2 c. chopped pecans

In a heavy saucepan over medium heat, stir sugar, water and salt
until sugar dissolves. Boil until mixture reaches the soft-ball stage,
or 234 to 243 degrees on a candy thermometer. Remove from heat.
Gradually pour 1/3 of corn syrup over egg whites and beat together.
Cook remaining syrup to hard ball stage, or 250 to 269 degrees. Beat
egg white mixture into hot syrup mixture until it holds shape. Stir in
nuts, if using. Drop by teaspoonfuls onto wax paper. Store in an
airtight container. Makes 4 dozen.

An old-fashioned candy-making hint...a cold, sunny winter
day is perfect weather for making candy. Don't try to
prepare homemade candy on a rainy or humid day,
as it may not set up properly.

Mincemeat Cookies

Rebecca Kelly
Marion, IN

These cookies will go fast! They're especially delicious warm, right out of the oven.

1 c. shortening
1-1/2 c. sugar
3 eggs, beaten
3 c. all-purpose flour
1 t. baking soda

1/2 t. salt
9-oz. pkg. condensed
   mincemeat, crumbled
Optional: vanilla frosting

In a large bowl, beat shortening and sugar until fluffy. Add eggs, beating well. Stir together flour, baking soda and salt; gradually add to shortening mixture. Mix well; stir in mincemeat. Drop by rounded teaspoonfuls, 2 inches apart, onto greased baking sheets. Bake at 375 degrees for 8 to 10 minutes, or until lightly golden. Cool; frost if desired. Makes about 6-1/2 dozen.

I plead for memories of olden times, and simple pleasures, and the making of the most delightful music in the world, the laughter of happy children...God bless us all and make us contented. Merry Christmas!
–A.M. Hopkins

Cookies by the Dozen

Honey Jumbles

Katie Majeske
Denver, PA

My Grandma Franz had a back room off her kitchen with a shelf of old-fashioned glass cookie jars. When I went to visit her, checking out the jars of cookies was better than going to a candy store! This recipe is so special to me because she gave me a handwritten copy of it. She passed away almost 35 years ago, but she gave me so many wonderful memories.

3-1/2 c. all-purpose flour,
   divided
1 c. sugar
2 t. baking soda

1/2 t. salt
1 c. honey
3 eggs, beaten
1 t. vanilla or anise extract

Stir together one cup flour, sugar, baking soda and salt. Add honey, eggs, extract and remaining flour; mix well. Cover and refrigerate overnight. Roll into 1-1/2 inch balls, flouring hands often. Place on lightly greased baking sheets. Bake at 325 degrees for about 15 minutes. Makes 3 dozen.

Fill icing cones with small candies or cookies, tie with colorful curling ribbons and tuck into a wire cupcake holder.
A clever way to display treats for take-home gifts!

Fruit & Nut Gems

Regina Kostyu
Delaware, OH

With applesauce, cranberries and walnuts, these chocolatey
nuggets are almost good for you!

12-oz. pkg. semi-sweet
   chocolate chips
1 c. applesauce
1 t. almond extract
3 c. powdered sugar

2/3 c. sweetened, dried
   cranberries, chopped
1-1/2 c. walnuts, finely chopped
   and divided

Combine chocolate chips, applesauce and extract in a large microwave-safe container. Microwave for 2 to 3 minutes on high setting until chocolate melts, stirring every 30 seconds. Stir until smooth. Add powdered sugar, cranberries and one cup walnuts; stir until well-mixed. Chill in refrigerator until firm enough to shape, about one hour. Scoop up mixture by teaspoonfuls and roll into balls; roll in remaining walnuts to coat. Keep refrigerated in an airtight container up to one week. Let stand at room temperature for about 30 minutes before serving. Makes about 3 dozen.

An old-fashioned lunch box is a perfect container to fill with
homemade cookies and candies...a great teacher gift too!

Cookies by the Dozen

Snowstorm Hard Candy

Marcia Bills
Orleans, NE

My 3 daughters always ask to make this at least once every winter during a snowstorm. It's great fun to make...they love to hear that cracking sound when the cold pan hits the snow! Maple, cinnamon and butter rum are some flavors they especially like.

3-1/2 c. sugar
1 c. light corn syrup
1 c. water

1 t. favorite candy flavoring oil
few drops food coloring

Grease a heavy metal baking sheet; dust with powdered sugar and set aside. Mix together sugar, corn syrup and water in a heavy saucepan. Cook over medium heat until mixture reaches the hard-crack stage, or 290 to 310 degrees on a candy thermometer. Remove from heat. Stir in flavoring oil and food coloring until desired shade is reached. Take pan outside and set on the snow, somewhere flat like a sidewalk. Using potholders, pour the extremely hot candy onto prepared baking sheet. Candy will cool quickly. Break into bite-size pieces. Store in an airtight container. Makes 4 cups.

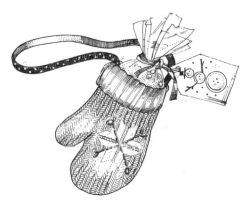

A pair of woolly mittens make a useful gift long after the
goodies have been enjoyed. Stitch a simple snowflake
pattern on a pair of blue mittens with white yarn
and tuck packaged Snowstorm Hard Candy inside.

Cranberry Wafers

Sandy Chandler
Champaign, IL

*We love these thin, flavorful cookies...they're delicious
with a hot cup of after-dinner coffee.*

1-1/4 c. sugar
1/2 c. margarine, softened
1/2 c. fat-free orange yogurt
2 egg whites, beaten
1/2 t. vanilla extract
1 c. sweetened dried
  cranberries, chopped

2 c. quick or long-cooking
  oats, uncooked
1-1/2 c. all purpose flour
1 t. baking powder
1/2 t. baking soda
1/4 c. powdered sugar

In a large bowl, beat sugar and margarine until creamy. Add yogurt,
egg whites, vanilla and cranberries; beat well and set aside. Combine
oats, flour, baking powder and baking soda in a separate bowl.
Gradually add to cranberry mixture; stir well. Cover and chill for
one to 3 hours. With lightly floured hands, shape dough into one-inch
balls. Place 3 inches apart on baking sheets that have been sprayed
with non-stick vegetable spray. Flatten to 1/8-inch thickness with
the bottom of a glass dipped in sugar. Bake at 375 degrees for 10 to
12 minutes, or until edges are lightly golden. Cool for 2 minutes on
baking sheets; remove to wire rack. Sift powdered sugar over warm
cookies; cool completely. Store in a tightly covered container. Makes
about 4 dozen.

Package a gift of cookies in a jiffy! Decorate a cardboard
mailing tube with stickers or cut-outs and slide
in a plastic-wrapped stack of cookies.

Cookies by the Dozen

Cherry Peek-a-Boos

Wendy Lee Paffenroth
Pine Island, NY

These are wonderful with your morning coffee! Try making them with apple pie filling and a dash of cinnamon too.

6 eggs, divided
1/2 c. butter, softened
2 c. sugar
1 t. vanilla extract
1 t. almond extract
3 c. all-purpose flour

2 t. baking powder
1/4 t. lemon zest
1/2 c. sour cream
21-oz. can cherry pie filling
Optional: 1/2 c. milk

Place 4 eggs, butter, sugar and extracts in a large bowl; beat well until blended. Add flour, baking powder and zest; blend in sour cream. Batter will be very thick. Spread 2/3 of batter in greased 13"x9" baking pan. Spoon pie filling over batter in pan. Carefully spread out and set aside. Blend remaining eggs into remaining batter. If batter is still very thick, add a little milk until batter is almost pourable. Pour batter over pie filling. With a knife, cut back and forth through mixture in pan. Bake at 350 degrees for 40 to 60 minutes. Cool and slice into bars. Makes 15 bars.

Add some whimsy to a wintertime gathering. Before guests arrive, fill a punch bowl with clean, fresh snow and nestle punch cups inside to chill. Guests can grab a cup and fill with soda or punch...it's sure to stay extra cool!

Martha Washingtons

Renee Velderman
Hopkins, MI

An old-fashioned chocolate candy that's chock-full of coconut, nuts and creamy milk...yum! Even if my mom doesn't make any other Christmas candy, she must make this one to please her children.

1 c. butter, melted and cooled
14-oz. can sweetened
    condensed milk
2 c. powdered sugar
2 c. pecans or walnuts, chopped

14-oz. pkg. sweetened flaked
    coconut
20-oz. pkg. melting chocolate,
    chopped

Combine all ingredients except chocolate; mix well and chill overnight. Roll into balls the size of marbles; set on wax paper-lined baking sheets or trays. Chill overnight again. Melt chocolate in a double boiler. Dip balls into chocolate and return to wax paper to cool. Makes about 6 dozen.

A chocolate truffle tree..how irresistible! Simply use toothpicks
to attach truffles or fudge candies to a styrofoam cone
until the cone is completely covered.

Cookies by the Dozen

Penuche

Jo Ann
Gooseberry Patch

*A rich-tasting fudge recipe that's made in a microwave...
what could be easier?*

2 c. brown sugar, packed
5-oz. can evaporated milk
1/2 c. butter

2 c. powdered sugar
1 t. vanilla extract

Combine brown sugar, evaporated milk and butter in a microwave-safe container. Microwave on high setting for 10 minutes, stirring frequently. Let stand for 5 minutes. Add powdered sugar and vanilla; stir until almost set. Pour into a lightly greased 9"x9" baking pan. Cool; cut into squares. Makes 2 to 3 dozen.

Who wouldn't like to receive her very own little pot of fudge?
Pour hot fudge into shallow plastic food storage containers
with snap-on lids and chill. Be sure to tuck in a small plastic
knife so the lucky recipient can indulge right away.

Totos

Melody Valente
San Jose, CA

My Nani (Italian for grandmother) was amazing in the kitchen. I wanted to get her recipes to make myself, but she never wrote anything down or even measured. "How much do I put, Nani?" "Oh, a pinch of that, just enough of this." We made these together several times before I got the whole recipe for these wonderful chocolate balls. We had so much fun... I think her secret ingredient was love!

3 c. all-purpose flour
1 c. sugar
1 T. baking powder
1/8 t. salt
1/4 c. baking cocoa
1/2 t. ground cloves

Optional: 1/2 t. cinnamon
3/4 c. shortening
2 eggs, beaten
1 T. vanilla extract
1 c. chopped nuts
1/3 c. milk

Sift flour, sugar, baking powder, salt, cocoa and spices together; mix well. Combine shortening, eggs and vanilla in a separate bowl; blend thoroughly. Slowly add flour mixture and nuts to shortening mixture. Gradually add milk until a soft dough forms (dough shouldn't be sticky). Roll into one-inch balls and place on ungreased baking sheets. Bake at 350 degrees for 10 minutes, or until golden on the bottom. Makes 4 dozen.

A quick & easy sampler of goodies! Arrange ruffled paper candy cups in a vintage tin and fill each with a different treat. Try an assortment including fudge balls, sugar-coated nuts and bite-size cookies...yum!

Cookies by the Dozen

Sand Tarts

Kristin Moore
Frostburg, MD

*My Grandma Miller always made this recipe at Christmastime.
It was an untraditional cookie but always a hit...
the recipe makes enough for a crowd too!*

1-1/2 c. butter
2 c. sugar
3 eggs, beaten
1/2 t. baking soda
1/2 t. water

5 c. all-purpose flour
1 egg white, beaten
Garnish: cinnamon-sugar
   to taste
Optional: chopped walnuts

Blend butter and sugar in a large bowl; add eggs. Dissolve baking
soda in water and add; mix in all-purpose flour. Form dough into
two, 1-1/2 inch diameter rolls; wrap and chill overnight. Slice dough
thinly and place on ungreased baking sheets. Brush cookies with egg
white and sprinkle with cinnamon-sugar. Walnuts can be added to
dough if desired. Bake at 375 degrees for 8 minutes. Makes about
7 dozen.

Show off tiny ornaments on a mini table-top tree all their own...
the size is perfect for a kitchen windowsill.

Old-Fashioned Cream Fondant

Mary Linda Wright
Farr West, UT

Grandma & Grandpa always had store-bought candy when we got together on Sunday evenings with our cousins, but her homemade fondant was best of all...definitely a comfort candy!

2 c. sugar
1 T. light corn syrup

1-1/2 c. whipping cream
1 t. vanilla extract

Combine sugar, corn syrup and cream in a heavy saucepan over medium heat. Cook, stirring constantly, until mixture reaches soft-ball stage, or 234 to 240 degrees on a candy thermometer, brushing down sides of pan often with a pastry brush moistened with warm water. Add vanilla; beat by hand until fondant loses its gloss. Form into one 12-inch roll, about 2 inches in diameter; wrap in aluminum foil and refrigerate for one hour. Cut into 1/2-inch pieces. Makes about 2 dozen.

Wrap individual squares of old-fashioned candy in wax paper and give in a jadite glass bowl...sure to bring back memories of Mom's kitchen.

Gifts
in Good Taste

Cranberry Nut Bread

Paula Wilson
Columbia, MO

I grew up attending a small rural church where it was customary to go caroling the week before Christmas. The best part was always returning to the church, where we warmed up with cups of hot chocolate and some of the best fruit breads and cookies ever made! My mother's Cranberry Nut Bread was always a favorite.

2 c. all-purpose flour
1 c. sugar
1-1/2 t. baking powder
1/2 t. baking soda
1 t. salt
1 t. orange zest

1 egg, beaten
2 T. oil
3/4 c. orange juice
1-1/4 c. cranberries, chopped
1/2 c. chopped pecans

Combine flour, sugar, baking powder, baking soda, salt and zest in a large bowl. Beat together egg, oil and juice in a separate bowl; add to dry ingredients and mix well. Stir in berries and nuts; set aside. Grease the bottom only of one, 9"x5" loaf pan or two, 7-1/2"x3-1/2" medium loaf pans. Pour batter into pans. Bake at 350 degrees, one hour for a regular loaf or 45 minutes for medium loaves. Turn out bread and cool on a wire rack. Makes one loaf or 2 medium loaves.

A loaf of homemade fruit bread is always a welcome gift! Make sure it stays fresh and tasty...let the bread cool completely before wrapping well in plastic wrap or aluminum foil.

Gifts in Good Taste

Pistachio Bread

Susie Pechtl
Fargo, ND

My neighbor was kind enough to share this recipe with me.
It is one of the best quick breads I've ever tasted!

18-1/2 oz. pkg. yellow cake mix
3.4-oz. pkg. instant pistachio
   pudding mix
8-oz. container sour cream
4 eggs, beaten

1/4 c. oil
1/4 c. water
6 T. brown sugar, packed
1 t. cinnamon
1/4 c. chopped nuts

Mix together dry cake and pudding mixes in a large bowl. Stir in
sour cream, eggs, oil and water; mix well. Pour into two, greased
9"x5" loaf pans or eight, 4-1/2"x2 1/2" mini loaf pans; set aside.
Combine brown sugar, cinnamon and nuts; sprinkle over loaves.
Bake at 350 degrees, 30 to 35 minutes for regular loaves or 17 to
20 minutes for mini loaves. Cool on wire racks for 5 to 10 minutes;
remove from pan. Makes 2 regular loaves or 8 mini loaves.

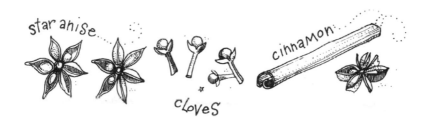

Mix up some kitchen potpourri. Combine a few tablespoons
each of whole spices like cloves, allspice, star anise, cardamom,
cinnamon sticks and whole nutmeg, breaking up any larger
pieces. Add dried orange or lemon peel if desired. Place
in a shallow bowl or fill a jar to give as a gift.

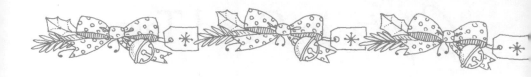

Cranberry-Orange Marmalade

Lois Bruce
Huntsville, AL

My friends just love to receive gift jars of this easy-to-make marmalade!
It's delicious on biscuits or homemade rolls, stirred into a bowl of
hot oatmeal or even used as a glaze on a baked ham steak.

32-oz. jar orange marmalade
12-oz. pkg. cranberries

6 1/2-pint canning jars and
lids, sterilized

Spoon marmalade into a microwave-safe 2-quart bowl; set aside.
Coarsely chop cranberries with a food chopper; add to marmalade and
mix well. Cover and microwave on high for 6 minutes, stirring and
covering again after 2 and 4 minutes. Spoon into hot sterilized jars,
leaving 1/4-inch headspace. Wipe rims; secure with lids and rings.
Process in a boiling water bath for 10 minutes; set jars on a towel to
cool. Check for seals. Store in refrigerator up to one year. Makes 5 to
6 jars.

Decorate a jar of homemade preserves in an instant with a
paper muffin cup liner in a festive holiday design. Simply
flatten the liner and place it design-side up on top of the
jar, pressing it down around the lid. Tie in place with
a narrow ribbon or jute. It's ready to give in no time.

Gifts in Good Taste

Lemon Curd

Jennifer Niemi
Meadowvale, Nova Scotia

*The sweet-tart flavor of homemade lemon curd is
really delicious on fresh-baked scones.*

1/2 c. butter
1-2/3 c. sugar
juice and zest of 4 lemons,
   divided

4 eggs, beaten
2 1/2-pint canning jars and
   lids, sterilized

Melt butter in a double boiler over hot water. Add sugar, lemon juice
and eggs; mix well. Stir in lemon zest. Cook, stirring constantly, until
thickened, about 15 minutes. Remove top of double boiler from heat;
cool slightly. Pour into hot sterilized jars, leaving 1/4-inch headspace.
Wipe rims; secure jar lids. Keep refrigerated for up to one week. Makes
2 jars.

Tuck a jar of Lemon Curd into a gift basket of extra-special
scones. Stir up a favorite scone recipe or mix, pat out the
dough and cut out with a heart-shaped cookie cutter.

Amish Friendship Bread

Mary Gentry
Pikeville, KY

My sister in Wisconsin gave me this recipe...here in Kentucky it has become a favorite for welcoming someone new to the community. Give the loaf away with a sweet friendship card that provides the recipe, so that more friends can enjoy.

4 c. sugar, divided
5 c. all-purpose flour, divided
3 c. milk, divided
1 c. sugar, divided
2/3 c. oil
3 eggs, beaten
2 t. vanilla extract

1-1/4 t. baking powder
1-1/2 t. baking soda
2 t. salt
Optional: 1/2 cup raisins,
    chopped walnuts and/or
    applesauce

Day 1: Make your starter. In a large bowl, mix one cup sugar, one cup flour and one cup milk using a wooden spoon. Place uncovered bowl in pantry; don't refrigerate. *Days 2, 3 and 4:* Stir once a day with a wooden spoon. *Day 5:* Add one cup sugar, one cup flour and one cup milk. Stir with a wooden spoon. *Days 6, 7, 8 and 9:* Stir once a day with a wooden spoon. *Day 10:* Add one cup sugar, one cup flour and one cup milk; stir with wooden spoon. Pour one cup starter into 4 glass or plastic containers. Attach complete instructions (along with a note to start at *Day 2*) and give to 3 friends, keeping one for yourself. To the remaining starter in the bowl, add remaining cup of sugar, remaining 2 cups of flour and other ingredients; mix well. Pour into a well greased and sugared 9"x5" loaf pan. Bake at 350 degrees for 40 to 50 minutes; check for doneness with a toothpick. Let cool 10 minutes before removing from pan. Makes 4 starters and one freshly baked loaf.

Gifts in Good Taste

Wildwood Pancake Mix

Holly Ledingham
Plainfield, IL

For more than 65 years, this recipe has been a staple on the menu of Wildwood Lodge in Northern Ontario, Canada, where my grandmother, Edythe Ashcroft, was once the head cook. Her scrumptious cooking drew generations of families back to this beautiful vacation spot year after year.

4 c. all-purpose flour
4 c. cracked wheat flour
1 c. sugar

2 T. baking powder
2 t. salt
1 c. lard

Combine all dry ingredients except lard; mix well. Cut in lard with a pastry cutter until well blended. Place in an airtight container; attach the following instructions. Makes about 10 cups mix.

Instructions:

Place 2 cups mix in a medium bowl. Add one beaten egg and 1-1/2 cups water to desired consistency; stir until moistened. Heat a buttered skillet over medium high heat. Pour 1/4 cup batter into skillet for each pancake. Cook pancakes until air bubbles appear on top; flip and cook other side. Serve pancakes topped with a pat of butter and warm maple syrup. Makes about 10 pancakes.

A cheerful yellowware bowl is a perfect container for a gift of Wildwood Pancake Mix. Tuck in a new pancake turner and bottle or two of fruit-flavored pancake syrup...yum!

Brandy Sauce

Rogene Rogers
Bemidji, MN

*Years ago we received a jar of this sauce as a Christmas gift. We loved
it so much as a topping for ice cream that we had to ask for the recipe.
Now we give jars of Brandy Sauce and all our recipients ask us for the
recipe...well, here it is!*

1 c. sugar	1 egg, beaten
1/3 c. water	1/4 c. brandy
2 T. butter	Optional: 2 T. lemon juice

In a small saucepan over medium heat, simmer sugar and water
together for about 5 minutes. Remove from heat; add butter and
stir until melted. Stir in beaten egg and blend thoroughly; heat to
boiling point, stirring constantly. Remove from heat; add remaining
ingredients and mix well. Pour into a decorative jar for gift giving.
Store in refrigerator up to 2 weeks. Makes 12 servings.

Keep an eye open at tag sales and flea markets for decorative
glass bottles and jars to fill with homemade food gifts.
Add a little white vinegar to the rinse water
after washing...they'll be sparkling!

Gifts in Good Taste

Vanilla & Cream Syrup

Jill Ball
Highland, UT

*My family likes breakfast so much that we often have breakfast
for dinner! This is one of our favorite syrups...we enjoy it
on pancakes, waffles and French toast.*

1 qt. maple syrup
14-oz. can sweetened
  condensed milk

1 T. cinnamon
3/4 t. nutmeg
1-1/2 t. vanilla extract

Mix all ingredients together; pour into a covered container. Keep
refrigerated up to 2 weeks. Makes about 5 cups.

English Rum Butter

Gloria Costes
West Hills, CA

*My grandmother brought this recipe to America many years ago.
A spoonful on hot toast makes it a delightful treat...just imagine
how wonderful it is on mince pies, fruitcake or bread pudding!*

6 T. rum extract
6 T. water
2 16-oz. pkgs. powdered sugar

1-1/2 t. cinnamon
1-1/2 t. nutmeg
1 c. butter, softened

Mix together extract and water; set aside. Combine powdered sugar
and spices in a large bowl. Gradually add butter and extract mixture;
blend well. Spoon into jars. Store in refrigerator up to one month.
Makes 3 to 4 jars.

Extra-special gift tags are easy. Glue snippets of rick rack,
buttons or scrapbooking charms to plain
card-stock tags...happy creating!

Zippy Pepper Jelly

Judy Awe
Lincoln, IL

I use green or red bell peppers for Christmas jelly, yellow peppers for springtime and bright orange peppers for fall...they all taste great.

1 c. green, red, yellow or orange pepper, finely chopped
1/2 c. jalapeño pepper, finely chopped
5 c. sugar
1-1/2 c. cider vinegar
6-oz. pkg. liquid pectin
5 to 6 1/2-pint canning jars and lids, sterilized

Combine peppers, sugar and vinegar in an 8 to 10-quart saucepan. Bring to a rolling boil over high heat; boil for 3 to 4 minutes. Remove from heat; let cool for 5 minutes. Add pectin, stirring constantly. Let mixture cool for 2 minutes, stirring to make sure pectin is mixed well. Pour into hot sterilized jars, leaving 1/4-inch headspace. Wipe rims; secure with lids and rings. Process for 5 minutes in a boiling water bath; set jars on a towel to cool. Check for seals; attach instructions. Makes 5 to 6 jars.

Zippy Pepper Jelly Spread:

Add 2 to 3 tablespoons of Zippy Pepper Jelly to a softened 8-ounce package of cream cheese. Blend with an electric mixer on low speed. Keep chilled; serve with crackers and fresh veggies.

Line a basket with a red bandanna and tuck in a jar of Zippy Pepper Jelly, a box of gourmet snack crackers and a small spreader. Two or three dried red chile peppers make a fun tie-on...they'll love it!

Gifts in Good Taste

Ruby Wine Jelly

Kendall Hale
Lynn, MA

*Tuck a jar of this yummy jelly and a box of crisp crackers
into a napkin-lined basket for a lovely hostess gift.*

3-1/2 c. red wine
1/2 c. lemon juice
1-3/4 oz. pkg. powdered pectin

4-1/2 c. sugar
5 to 6 1/2-pint canning jars
   and lids, sterilized

Combine wine, lemon juice and pectin in a large saucepan over
medium heat. Bring to a boil, stirring frequently. Add sugar; stir until
dissolved. Return to a rolling boil; boil hard for one minute, stirring
constantly. Remove from heat; quickly skim off any foam. Spoon into
hot sterilized jars, leaving 1/4-inch headspace. Wipe rims; secure with
lids and rings. Process for 5 minutes in a boiling water bath; set jars
on a towel to cool. Check for seals. Makes 5 to 6 jars.

Cranberry Chutney

Tena Stollar
Kensington, OH

*I make this family favorite as soon as the first fresh cranberries
appear in the fall. It's a must with any holiday ham or turkey!*

2 c. cranberries
2 c. sugar
3 T. water
1 apple, cored, peeled and
   chopped
2 stalks celery, chopped

1 T. orange zest
1 c. orange juice
1 c. golden raisins
1/2 t. ground ginger
1/4 t. ground cloves

Combine cranberries, sugar and water in a medium saucepan. Cook
over medium heat for 5 minutes. Add remaining ingredients. Cook
stirring often for 35 minutes. Remove from heat, chill if desired. Keep
refrigerated up to 3 weeks. Makes 2-1/2 cups.

Sugar & Spice Almonds

Angie O'Keefe
Soddy Daisy, TN

Yummy...just as good as the nuts we crave at the county fair!

3/4 c. sugar
1 T. Sweet Spice Blend
3/4 t. salt

1 egg white
1 T. water
1 lb. almonds or pecan halves

Combine sugar, one tablespoon spice blend and salt in a medium bowl; set aside. Beat egg white in a separate bowl until foamy, using a whisk or an electric mixer on medium speed. Add nuts to egg white, stirring until coated evenly. Turn nuts into sugar mixture, stirring until evenly coated. Spread in an even layer on a buttered 15"x10" jelly-roll pan. Bake at 275 degrees for 50 to 55 minutes, stirring every 15 minutes. Spread on wax paper to cool. Makes 8 servings.

Sweet Spice Blend:

2 T. light brown sugar, packed
4 T. ground ginger
2-1/2 T. cinnamon

1 t. nutmeg
1/2 t. ground cloves

Mix all ingredients; store in a small jar.

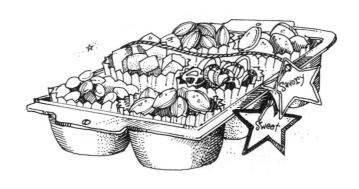

Gifts in Good Taste

Honey Popcorn & Cashews

Diane Garber
Brookville, OH

*This recipe came from a dear neighbor, when we first moved to
our new home in 1977. My 3 sons just loved it.
It is very addictive and always a hit.*

3 qts. popped popcorn
1-1/2 c. cashews
1 c. sugar
1/2 c. honey

1/2 c. light corn syrup
1 c. creamy peanut butter
1 t. vanilla extract

Toss together popped corn and nuts in a large roaster pan; keep warm
in a 250-degree oven. In a heavy 1-1/2 quart saucepan, combine
sugar, honey and corn syrup. Bring mixture to a boil over medium
heat, stirring constantly. Boil hard for 2 minutes. Remove from heat;
stir in peanut butter and vanilla. Immediately pour over popcorn
mixture, stirring to coat thoroughly. Spread on aluminum foil to cool.
Break into bite-size pieces. Makes 3 quarts.

A little smile, a word of cheer,
A bit of love from someone near,
A little gift from one held dear,
Best wishes for the coming year.
– John Greenleaf Whittier

White Chocolate Popcorn

Patty Fosnight
Childress, TX

Sprinkle with colored sugar or candy jimmies in holiday colors.

5 to 6 pkgs. butter-flavored
   microwave popcorn, popped
24-oz. pkg. white melting
   chocolate, chopped

6 1.4-oz. white chocolate
   crunch candy bars, chopped

Pour popcorn into a large bowl, removing any unpopped kernels.
Combine chocolates in a large heavy saucepan over low heat. Cook
and stir until melted and smooth. Pour over popcorn and mix well.
Spread out on wax paper to cool. Package in small bags for gift
giving. Makes 20 to 24 servings.

A gift your best girlfriend will love! Fill a pink cellophane bag
with White Chocolate Popcorn and add a copy of a
paperback book she's been wanting to read.

Gifts in Good Taste

Cinnamon Peanut Brittle

Jennifer Oglesby
Brownsville, IN

*I make this simple recipe every year for Christmas and it's
a huge hit...you'll never eat ordinary peanut brittle again!*

1 c. sugar
1/2 c. light corn syrup
2 c. salted peanuts
1 t. butter

1/2 t. cinnamon
1 t. baking soda
1 t. vanilla extract

Combine sugar and corn syrup in a 2-quart microwave-safe glass
container. Cook, uncovered, on high for 4 minutes; stir. Heat
3 minutes longer; stir in peanuts, butter and cinnamon. Cook,
uncovered, on high for 30 to 60 seconds or until mixture turns a light
amber color. Mixture will be very hot. Quickly stir in baking soda and
vanilla until light and foamy. Immediately pour onto a greased baking
sheet and spread with a metal spatula. Refrigerate for 20 minutes or
until firm; break into pieces. Store in an airtight container. Makes
1-1/4 pounds.

A snowman kit...all ready for the first big snowfall!
Fill a big box with a woolly scarf, hat and mittens
(hand-me-downs or thrift-store finds are perfect).
Add some button eyes...tuck in a camera to catch the fun!

5-Minute Fudge Wreaths

Mary Lyhane
Marysville, KS

This fudge makes a wonderful Christmas gift for friends & neighbors...
they never suspect how easy it is to make either!

14-oz. can sweetened
  condensed milk
12-oz. pkg. bittersweet
  chocolate chips
1 c. butterscotch chips

1 t. vanilla extract
8-oz. pkg. chopped walnuts
1/2 c. raisins
Garnish: red and green candied
  cherries

Pour condensed milk into a medium saucepan; set aside. Rinse out
empty can; cover can completely with plastic wrap. Place can in the
center of a buttered 8" round cake pan; set aside. Add chocolate chips,
butterscotch chips and vanilla to condensed milk. Cook and stir over
low heat until chocolate melts, about 3 minutes. Stir in nuts and
raisins. Scoop warm fudge into prepared cake pan around wrapped
can to form a ring or wreath shape, pushing can back into center if it
moves. Smooth top of fudge. Decorate fudge wreath with several
groups of holly berry sprigs, using halved red cherries for holly berries
and quartered green cherries for holly leaves. Chill until firm. Discard
can; loosen the sides and bottom of the fudge with a spatula. Wrap in
plastic wrap; secure with a bow or ornament, if desired. Makes one
wreath, about 2 pounds.

Round up small nostalgic toys and dolls
and use them to trim a mini Christmas
tree. Tie toys to the branches with
brightly colored yarn...so charming!

Gifts in Good Taste

Graham Cracker Fudge

Nancy Otto
Indiana, PA

My mother wrote down her favorite fudge recipe for me on lined tablet paper the first Christmas I was married (over 40 years ago!). She saved the original clipping in her recipe file too, cut from the November 1942 issue of Woman's Day magazine. Now I have both copies...they are yellowed with time, but the fudge is as delicious and chewy as ever.

2 sqs. unsweetened baking
   chocolate
14-oz. can sweetened
   condensed milk
1/2 t. vanilla extract

1-3/4 c. graham crackers,
   finely crushed
1-1/2 c. chopped pecans,
   walnuts or almonds, divided
1 t. butter

Melt chocolate in a double boiler over hot water. Add condensed milk and cook, stirring constantly, until mixture thickens, about 5 minutes. Add vanilla, graham cracker crumbs and one cup nuts; mix well. Butter an 8"x8" baking pan and sprinkle half the remaining nuts in the bottom. Spread chocolate mixture in pan, using a knife that has been dipped in hot water. Press remaining nuts into top. Cover with plastic wrap and chill overnight. Cut into squares. Makes 16 to 20 pieces.

For an invitation to chat any time, tuck a phone card
into a gift box filled with Graham Cracker Fudge.

Fiesta Dip Mix

Jo Ann
Gooseberry Patch

*Add other seasonings like garlic, cayenne pepper or Mexican
oregano to create your very own dip mix.*

1/2 c. dried parsley
1/3 c. dried, minced onion
1/3 c. chili powder

1/4 c. ground cumin
1/4 c. dried chives
Optional: 1/4 c. salt

Combine all ingredients and mix well. Spoon into a jar; attach
instructions. Makes about 2 cups mix.

Instructions:

Combine 3 tablespoons dip mix with one cup mayonnaise and one cup
sour cream or plain yogurt. Whisk until smooth, adding more dip mix
to taste, if desired. Chill for 4 hours to overnight, to allow flavors to
blend. Serve with tortilla or corn chips. Makes 2 cups dip.

Tie a bag of fresh, homemade tortilla chips to a jar of Fiesta
Dip Mix for a tasty gift! Spray corn tortilla wedges lightly with
non-stick vegetable spray and bake at 375 degrees for 7 to
10 minutes until crispy. Choose red tortillas for a fun twist.

Gifts in Good Taste

Taste of Italy Seasoning

Tina Wright
Atlanta, GA

This versatile mix is even good sprinkled on buttered popcorn!

1/3 c. dried oregano	1 T. garlic powder
1/4 c. dried basil	1 t. dried rosemary
1/4 c. dried parsley	1 t. salt
3 T. dried sage	

Combine all ingredients. Mix well and place in a small jar; attach instructions. Makes about one cup.

Zesty Roasted Potatoes:

Place 3 pounds quartered new potatoes in a plastic zipping bag; drizzle with 1/4 cup olive oil. Add one tablespoon seasoning mix and shake to coat well. Pour potatoes into an aluminum foil-lined 15"x10" jelly-roll pan. Bake at 450 degrees for 30 minutes or until potatoes are tender, stirring once.

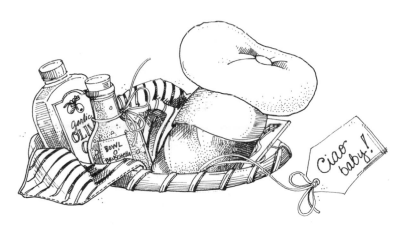

Fill up a tray or basket with spices, cooking tools and even an apron...slip in your own homemade food gift mix for a personal touch. They're sure to appreciate your thoughtfulness.

Simmering Soup Bags

Regina Wickline
Pebble Beach, CA

I make these flavorful packets with dried herbs from my garden.
Sometimes I'll use mini cheesecloth bags from a kitchen supply
store...just pop in the herbs and cinch the drawstring.

12 6-inch squares cheesecloth
1/4 c. dried parsley
1 T. dried thyme

1 T. dried tarragon
12 bay leaves
kitchen string

On each cheesecloth square, place one teaspoon parsley, 1/4 teaspoon thyme, 1/4 teaspoon tarragon and one bay leaf. Tie into bags with kitchen string. Place bags in a large canning jar. Makes one gift jar of 12 bags.

Instructions:

Add one bag to homemade vegetable soup, beef stew or spaghetti sauce during the last 30 minutes of cooking.

Wrap up a soup-making kit for a friend...perfect for cold winter weather. Fill an enamelware soup kettle with a jar of Simmering Soup Bags, a package of small soup pasta, a ladle and a stack of hearty soup mugs. A welcome gift for a frosty day.

Gifts in Good Taste

Spicy Cajun Rub

Kerry Mayer
Dunham Springs, LA

I like to pack this spice blend in mini glass shaker-top jars like pizza parlors use for grated Parmesan cheese...so handy!

1/4 c. paprika	1 T. white pepper
4 t. onion powder	1 t. pepper
4 t. garlic powder	2 t. dried thyme
4 t. cayenne pepper	2 t. dried oregano
4 t. salt	

Combine all ingredients in a bowl; mix well. Place in a small jar; attach instructions. Makes about 2/3 cup.

Instructions:

Sprinkle generously on pork chops or pork tenderloin before grilling or roasting. Excellent with fish too...sprinkle over fillets before pan-frying.

A special gift for a favorite cook...tuck a jar of
Spicy Cajun Rub into the pocket of
a new ruffled apron!

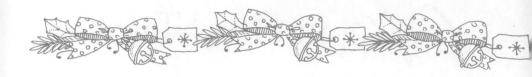

Puffy Caramel Corn

Cyndy DeStefano
Mercer, PA

Sunny, cold winter days are perfect for preparing this delectable concoction...it turns sticky when made in humid weather.

8-oz. pkg. hull-less popcorn
Optional: 1 c. cashews
1 c. butter, sliced
1 c. brown sugar, packed

1/2 c. light corn syrup
1 t. baking soda
Optional: 1/2 c. semi-sweet or
    white melting chocolate disks

Place popcorn and nuts, if using, in a large roaster pan that has been sprayed with non-stick vegetable spray; set aside. Combine butter, brown sugar and corn syrup in a heavy 2-quart saucepan; bring to a boil over medium heat. Boil for 2 minutes, stirring constantly. Add baking soda and stir until mixture foams. Pour caramel mixture over popcorn; stir until well coated. Bake at 250 degrees for 45 minutes, stirring every 10 to 15 minutes. Pour onto wax paper and break apart; let cool. If using, place chocolate disks in a microwave-safe bowl. Melt chocolate in microwave on high setting, stirring every 15 seconds until melted. Drizzle over popcorn; let cool. Store in large plastic zipping bags. Makes 12 servings.

Delight a movie buff! Fill a giant popcorn tin with a bag of Puffy Caramel Corn along with movie rental coupons and a movie magazine or two.

Gifts in Good Taste

"Ci-deer" Mulling Spices

Kelly Alderson
Erie, PA

*These sugar & spice-filled orange halves are so cute, and they make
the best-tasting mulled cider ever...a super gift tied to a small jug
of apple cider! My kids love to arrange the spices on top.*

3 oranges	6 whole nutmegs
1-1/8 c. brown sugar, packed	12 whole allspice
6 1-1/2 inch cinnamon sticks	48 whole cloves

Slice oranges in half; scoop out pulp without breaking the orange
peels. Reserve pulp for another use. Place each orange half on a
baking sheet, cut-side down over a small ball of aluminum foil. Bake
at 250 degrees for 2 hours, until hard and dry. Let cool completely.
Fill orange halves with brown sugar; pack firmly, mounding slightly.
Press spices into brown sugar to form a reindeer shape, using a
cinnamon stick for the body, a nutmeg for the head, 2 allspice for ears
(on either side of the head) and 6 to 8 cloves for the antlers and legs.
Wrap tightly with plastic wrap; attach instructions. Makes 6.

Instructions:

Pour 1-1/2 quarts apple cider into a saucepan. Unwrap the "Ci-deer"
and drop into cider. Simmer over low heat for 30 minutes. Strain
whole spices and orange rind from cider; serve hot.

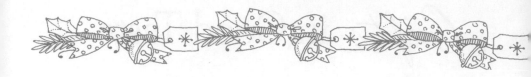

"Here, Kitty Kitty" Mist

Annette Forbes
East Ridge, TN

This simple spray mist turns any toy into a catnip-scented delight! Cats love valerian too, so for a variation, I like to combine 1/2 cup dried catnip with 1/2 cup dried valerian. You can buy both herbs at a health food store.

3 c. water   1 c. dried catnip

Bring water to a boil in a saucepan. Remove from heat and stir in catnip. Let steep for a hour or so or until cool. Strain into a spray bottle. Attach instructions: To use, spray mist on your cat's favorite toys or places to sleep. Keep refrigerated for one week. Makes about 3 cups.

Tie a fluffy yarn pompom onto a bottle of "Here, Kitty Kitty" Mist…an extra gift for a playful kitten!

Gifts in Good Taste

Doggie Crunchies

Edith Beck
Elk Grove, CA

*My own dog taste-tested these biscuits and was very happy with them!
So I bake lots to tuck into my Christmas cookie baskets for the dog
lovers on my list. I pack them in cute little cellophane bags with a
doggie design.*

2 eggs, beaten
1/2 c. canned pumpkin
1/2 t. salt

2 T. powdered milk
2-1/2 c. whole-wheat flour

Blend eggs and pumpkin; stir in salt, powdered milk and flour. If
dough is too crumbly, add just enough water to make it workable.
Roll or pat out dough on a floured surface; cut out biscuits with a
bone-shaped cookie cutter. Place on an ungreased baking sheet. Bake
at 350 degrees for 20 minutes; turn biscuits over and bake for an
additional 20 minutes. Makes about 1-1/2 dozen.

Turn a clear glass canister into a treat jar for your favorite pet!
Paint on bone shapes or pawprints and the pet's name
with acrylic permanent paint...it's so easy and
clean-up with water is a breeze.

Orange Pomander

Jennie Gist
Gooseberry Patch

These clove-studded fruits are fun for kids to do! Make them at Thanksgiving and enjoy their spicy scent throughout the Christmas holiday.

1-1/2 oz. jar whole cloves
1 orange

1 T. pumpkin pie spice
Optional: 1 t. orris root powder

Press cloves into the orange's peel, pointed ends down. Arrange cloves in swirls, lines or circles. A small awl can be used to pierce holes, if peel is especially thick or tough. Place spice in a small bowl; roll orange in spice mixture to coat. Orange will gradually dry out and can be kept indefinitely. Makes one pomander.

Dress up spicy orange pomanders with ribbon bows and heap them in a stoneware bowl...so sweet-smelling on a kitchen table.

Sweet
Memories

A Moonlit Sleigh Ride

Bethi Hendrickson
Danville, PA

In 1991, my husband was in Korea on a year's unaccompanied tour of duty and I had moved home to my parents' farm. My daddy had a team of mules and a wonderful bobsled, and one snow-covered night he invited me on a sleigh ride. We got all dressed up in our woolly warm clothing, harnessed the mules, climbed in and set out on our adventure. It had snowed all day, but now the sky was clear and the moon was full...you couldn't have asked for a more beautiful night! We headed up over the hill into the hay fields, enjoying the sounds of the sleigh. As we made the turn to come home, the mules stopped on the side hill and the sleigh flipped over, sending Daddy and me down the hill. Once the initial shock was over and we knew we were both all right, the laughter began. We must have been a sight to see...two big heaps of coats, scarves, mittens and boots! I think I even heard Polly and Jenny (the mules) laugh a little. We pushed the sleigh back up, climbed back in and headed home for a hot cup of coffee. Even after all these years, this memory still brings a tear to my eyes and a laugh to my heart.

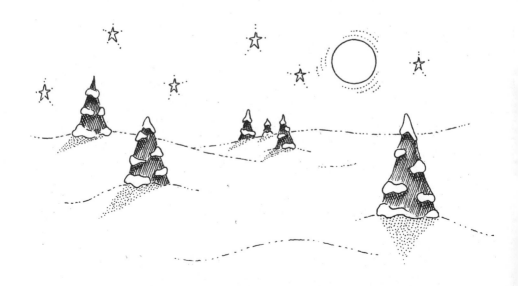

Sweet *Memories*

Milkshakes for Breakfast

Brenda Hurst
Greenwood, IN

Our family has had a unique Christmas tradition for almost 30 years.
Every Christmas morning after opening gifts, we share a big country
breakfast complete with bacon, sausage, eggs, hashbrowns, biscuits
and homemade jelly. But the most important thing on our menu is
chocolate milkshakes. That's right...chocolate milkshakes, made
from scratch and served with breakfast. These have become such a
tradition that our grown sons always call in advance to make sure
we have ice cream, milk and chocolate syrup on hand to make the
shakes. Christmas morning just would not be right in the Hurst
household without the chocolate milkshakes!

Magical Tree

Mary Sadler
Allen Park, MI

Back in the 1940's when my sister and I were little, we believed that
Santa decorated the Christmas tree on Christmas Eve when he came
to deliver our presents. Mom & Dad would put the lights on the tree,
but that was all. On Christmas morning, when we woke up, our
mother would guide us through the living room to the kitchen with a
scarf held over our eyes so we wouldn't see the tree or our presents.
When we had finished breakfast, she would open the door to the
living room, and what a beautiful sight it was...the decorated tree and
all our gifts underneath it! Mom & Dad must have stayed up all night
decorating it! This has always been one of my most cherished
Christmas memories.

Sweet Memories

Straw for the Creche

Kathy Blackburn
Spencerport, NY

On the first of December, my family would set up the creche with Mary, Joseph and all the other figures except the baby Jesus. Throughout the month, if we showed a kindness to others, did well in school or did something special, we could place a piece of straw in the baby's crib. The kids would rush home everyday to put their piece (or two!) of straw into the crib. On Christmas Eve we would lay the baby in the crib, which by then would be overflowing with straw. We kids loved this sweet tradition, which encouraged us to behave a little more like Jesus.

Cookie Decorating Time

Lori Krigbaum
Stoughton, WI

I have such fond Christmas memories of my sisters, brothers and myself (there are nine of us!) lining up at the kitchen table for cookie decorating time. Mom and my older sister would frost the cooled cut-outs and then pass them down the "assembly line," where each of us had our own containers of candy sprinkles or red cinnamon candies to apply. We were quite creative, but even more so when we turned the frosted cookies upside-down to gather up all the scattered sugars and sprinkles from the tabletop. Now, those were some well-decorated cookies...what a mess, but what fun we had! It still makes me smile.

205

A Moving Memory

Tari Carbaugh
Bartlesville, OK

My family's most special Christmas was in 2002. We were moving into our new country home in Oklahoma on December 23rd. That morning it started to snow heavily. The movers delivered the first truckload, then got stuck...they weren't able to deliver the rest of our stuff. We were amazed as we unpacked our small load. The movers couldn't have known they would get only one load to us, but Someone Else knew and took good care of us. The four twin mattresses from our kids' bunkbeds were delivered, along with a few chairs and the refrigerator. A box of kitchenware was delivered. One box even had a board game and playing cards. We also had bedding, towels and a coffeepot which we had packed in our car. Amazingly, it seemed all our needs were being met! On Christmas Eve, the electricity went out, but that wasn't a problem as we had unpacked a flashlight and some candles. We found one small box marked CHRISTMAS. In it, we discovered a small Christmas tree with tiny ornaments and lights on it. I don't know where this tree came from... I didn't recall ever having seen it before! The box also contained a nativity scene, the kids' Christmas stockings and an ornament that played Christmas carols. On Christmas Day we even found a disposable camera! A wonderful new neighbor invited us to Christmas dinner with their family. It was just the most blessed Christmas ever. Some might have focused on, and been disappointed about, the inconvenience. My family, however, felt the true meaning of Christmas with every blessing that we unpacked.

Sweet *Memories*

Santa's at My House!

Nancy Rhoades
Lebanon, MO

Years ago, we used to attend Christmas Eve services at a small country church. There was always such excitement and anticipation in young and old alike...when you walked in, you could just feel the spirit. The room was very small and always packed. After the Christmas play, the pastor invited everyone to stay for fellowship and refreshments. Then he added, "You know, I heard Santa Claus may stop and pay us a visit." Our almost 3-year-old son Lance stood up in the pew and shouted, "No he's not, he's at my house!" Needless to say, that's a Christmas we'll never forget!

An Italian Tradition

Lisa Ashton
Aston, PA

My father comes from a small town called Saint Vito in Calabria, Italy. His family celebrated on January 6th, the Feast of the Epiphany, rather than on Christmas Day. All the children would receive small trinkets such as fruit and nuts, some candies and perhaps a small toy. They always made sure that they celebrated the Wise Kings' search for Baby Jesus by setting up a precepio. It's a small mountain made out of paper maché made to look like the hills of Bethlehem. It's decorated with small houses, trees and lots of small animals, and trimmed with artificial snow. At the bottom of the mountain is the cave in which Jesus was born. My father continued this tradition as my brother and sister and I were growing up, and still continues it for his six grandchildren. It's always a joy to see the precepio through the eyes of our children as they search for Baby Jesus on the mountain.

Sweet *Memories*

A Caroling Hayride

Debra Collins
Gaylesville, AL

I love Christmas! I love everything about it. But I've noticed in the last few years that a lot of the holiday traditions have been forgotten. So last year I planned a Christmas caroling hayride for my family. Dressed up in his Santa Claus suit, my husband Steve hitched up his wagon to the tractor. We loaded it with hay and cozy quilts and off we went...Steve, myself, our three grown children, our four grandchildren, my sister and her son, and my 70-year-old mother. We sang our hearts out as we rode along. We forgot the words to some of the carols, so we just made them up as we went. It was very cold, but not one person complained...such a wonderful, magical night! At the end of the ride we came back in, gathered around the fireplace and talked about all of our Christmas plans. My children are already calling me asking to do it again this year. I do believe this is going to be one of our very own holiday traditions.

The Elf Gift

Karla Rush
Sherman, TX

When my children were quite young, I started our tradition of the elf gift. Every morning I would tie a small piece of candy, stickers, tiny toy or ornament to a little wooden elf figurine. I would then hide the elf somewhere in the house. When the children woke up, I would encourage them to look for the elf and his gift. Whoever found the elf got to keep the little gift, but in return they had to perform a good deed or kindness that day for someone else "to show gratitude for the elf gift." It was so much fun watching and helping my children come up with ways every day in December to give back some holiday cheer! Some days it was a special picture drawn with crayons and hidden under another's pillow or in their backpack or briefcase. Sometimes it was baking cookies and delivering them to the neighbors. Sometimes it would be shining Daddy's shoes, or cleaning all the mirrors in the house. Little chores weren't seen as chores, but as a return of the elf gift. My oldest child (who is 24 now) still remembers those days, and has asked for the wooden elf so that he can start his own elf gift tradition for his children.

Sweet *Memories*

The Christmas Wagon

Mary Therese Onoshko
Brick, NJ

Every year at Christmastime, the children and I bake dozens of cookies from recipes we pick out of one of our many **Gooseberry Patch** cookbooks. We make a special little craft that we have selected from one of the craft books, pack them together in special bags and deliver them via wagon throughout the neighborhood. When we started, we had just moved here and didn't know many people at all. Now our list is up to 19 and is growing every year. It's a great way for the children to recognize the importance of giving and reaching out to others...we've made a lot of new friends along the way too!

Grandmother's Grab Bags

Carol Svoboda
Lakewood, CO

When I was growing up, my Grandmother Svoboda would make "grab bags" for each of her children's families. Over the year, she saved the cardboard tubes from paper towels along with other small containers. Inside she would tape money...quarters, fifty-cent pieces and rolled-up dollar bills. We would have so much fun unwrapping all the little items. We would each end up with two or three dollars... when you're a kid, that's a fortune! The day after Christmas is my birthday, so we always went shopping then to spend my cash. Maybe this is why I still love unwrapping presents!

Sounds of the Season

Janie Reed
Gooseberry Patch

Ah, Christmas! For me the tradition of Christmas was always about Christmas Eve, when we would all pile into the car and head to Grandma's house. Grandma & Grandpa, all their children and grandchildren would gather in their modest home in the center of a small town. There was always lots of catching up and reminiscing along with plenty of finger foods. Heaven knows, with nearly 50 of us there was no way to have a sit-down meal! All the rooms were standing room only and we spilled over onto the front porch.

The highlight of the evening, however, was when we would all sing Christmas carols. Music was always a big part of our family activities and from the rich baritones and the melodic soprano voices to all the harmonies in between, everyone contributed their part. Many friends from the neighborhood would congregate on the porch and even set up lawn chairs to be closer to the music. It seemed to me like caroling in reverse.

The last song of the night was always "Jingle Bells." My grandmother never sought the limelight but on this night, after much begging from all of us, she would sing the verses solo with all of us joining in on the choruses. I remember how her voice would falter in the first few bars and then become stronger as she found her confidence. I know it took courage for her to do that, even though she was surrounded by her loved ones, and I admired her for doing it.

My grandparents are no longer with us, and the tradition they created has gone the way of so many others in the rush of completing less important tasks. My family has made our own traditions and they suit us, but in my heart, no tradition will ever come close to the magic of those Christmas Eves spent at Grandma's house.

Sweet *Memories*

A Family Christmas Play

Carolyn Lipham
Augusta, GA

When I married my husband in 1997, I joined a family that loves Christmas traditions! My most favorite tradition involves all my nieces & nephews. My mother-in-law has all her grandchildren act out the Christmas story. The oldest reads the story from the Bible and the younger ones take on the roles of Mary, Joseph, the three Wise Men and the Angel. This year my sister-in-law had a new baby and he was Baby Jesus. Our little play always puts the real meaning of Christmas into perspective and gets all of the children involved. My husband and I can't wait to have our own children and watch them take part in this wonderful family tradition.

A Little Note from Santa

Sherry Wampler
Roanoke, VA

When I was a child, on Christmas Eve we always served Santa cookies and coffee. I would proudly set them out, so excited. The next morning I would race down the stairs to see what Santa had left for me. After looking at all the wonderful things he had brought, I would check the cookies and coffee...wow! They were gone and there was a note on the plate. It read:

> *Thanks for the coffee and cookies.*
>
> *See you next year,*
>
> *Santa*

I was so very excited, I would carry the note around for days after Christmas. Years later, I found out that my sweet brother Bruce always came home after I was fast asleep, ate the cookies, tossed out the coffee (now very cold) and wrote me a note from Santa! I still have one of the notes today. I treasure this memory of a brother who took the time to make my Christmas special, even more so now since he is no longer with me.

214

Sweet *Memories*

A Birthday Cake for Jesus

Debby Rapp
Irmo, SC

Teaching young children the real meaning of Christmas, when Santa Claus is so prominent, was a goal that my husband and I wanted to accomplish with our two young sons. We began this ritual the Christmas that they were one and three years old. I baked a small cake and placed a candle on it. We sang "Happy Birthday" to Jesus and blew out the candle before viewing the Christmas tree and the presents. It became an annual tradition until they were young teens... they grew up knowing the true priority of the holiday in our home. Our sons are now 22 and 24 years old and still talk about the "Baby Jesus birthday cake" when they were small and the meaning that it had to them. I guess we accomplished our goal!

The Angel Tree

Korbi Slocum
Johnstown, PA

My best holiday memory relates to gift-giving. When my children, Breanne and Joshua, were little, I didn't want them growing up to be self-centered. So I began a holiday tradition. I had them pick a name, usually of a young child, from the "Angel Tree" at church. They both understood there would be one less present waiting for them under the tree. Instead, I would take the children shopping to buy gifts for our angel child. Watching the joy on their faces as they rushed around the store looking for the right presents touched me in a way that is hard to explain. They were so excited to know that they helped to make another child's Christmas brighter! In a world where people tend to put themselves first, my family is blessed by this tradition, which we've continued for more than 14 years now.

Christmas Crafts

Laura Hartman
Oswego, IL

Our family began a fun tradition about 10 years ago. My great-aunt had moved into a new condo, and she needed new Christmas ornaments. So she purchased plain glass ornaments in red, green and blue, and after Thanksgiving dinner, each of us...men, women and children painted Christmas scenes on them with acrylic paints. The fun and easy craft kept everyone from falling asleep after that turkey dinner. The following year, no one asked what was on the menu for Thanksgiving dinner, but everyone wanted to know about the Christmas craft. So, from that year forward, we have continued to begin the Christmas season with family & friends on Thanksgiving afternoon. The ornaments, bowls, sock snowmen and T-shirts bring us laughter and memories, but most importantly, bring us even closer as a family.

Sweet *Memories*

Measuring Up

Danielle Morris
Imperial, MO

When I was growing up, every Christmas my whole family would gather at my aunt & uncle's house to share gifts, food, and good times. After our big turkey dinner, the kids would all run around the house begging to open up gifts that Santa had magically left for us at their house. But we always knew that there was one thing we were to do before we could open gifts, and we all loved it! We would gather in the basement and my uncle would take down a piece of paneling from the wall. We lined up from youngest to oldest and took turns placing our backs against the wall to have our height measurement marked on the wall. It was so much fun standing in line with our cousins to see how much we had grown in the previous year! We would dance around and sing songs while everyone else was being measured. My uncle would then place the paneling back on the wall until next Christmas. Looking back, I think that was the best time of the day for me, being with my entire family and seeing just how much we had "grown up" in the past year. I am now 26 and starting my own family. I can't wait until I can continue the tradition of seeing how much my children have grown each year!

There Goes Santa!

Joy McCabe
Yorktown Heights, NY

My favorite memory happened when my daughter Maria was six and my son John was four. We live in the country and my parents, who are gone now, were visiting for the holidays. My mother came up with this wonderful idea. On Christmas morning, about 5:30 a.m., my husband dressed up in a Santa outfit. With only the Christmas tree lights lit, I snapped a Polaroid picture of Santa taking gifts from his sack, placing them under the Christmas tree and filling all the stockings. When he left, just at dawn, my parents and I woke the children. We all gathered in my son's room and looked out the window. I can still hear the children's shrieks of joy as they saw Santa Claus with his sack on his back, walking up our back hill into the woods. Halfway up, Santa turned around and waved to the children. I thought they would wake all the neighbors with their screams! My husband sneaked back into the house through the downstairs door, hid the Santa suit, and came upstairs in his PJ's asking what all the ruckus was about. The children were breathless, telling him about seeing Santa and showing him the picture. The funny thing is, they never did ask where he'd been. Years later, we still have that picture. My daughter can't wait until her own daughter Isabella is four, so she too can see Santa going up Nana & Poppy's hill into the woods.

Sweet *Memories*

A Family Scavenger Hunt

Mildred Trent
Elkview, WV

One Christmas when our grown children came to visit, I wanted to make it extra-special and fun. I thought of things that you might pack for a trip (toothbrush, shampoo, etc.) and wrote them down. I bought some inexpensive gifts and wrapped them. One night I told our grown kids that we were having a scavenger hunt. I explained that when I gave them the name of an item on the list, the first one to find it and bring it to me, would win a prize. You had to laugh to see these married adults racing around! That was four years ago and now every Christmas we each plan a game and buy little prizes for the winners...we love it!

INDEX

INDEX

INDEX

Since 1992, we've been publishing country cookbooks for every kitchen and for every meal of the day! Each has hundreds of budget friendly recipes, using ingredients you already have on hand. Their lay-flat binding makes them easy to use and each is filled with hand-drawn artwork and plenty of personality.

Send us your favorite recipe!

and the memory that makes it special for you!* If we select your recipe for a brand-new **Gooseberry Patch** cookbook, your name will appear right along with it...and you'll receive a FREE copy of the book.

Share your recipe on our website at
www.gooseberrypatch.com

Or mail to:

Gooseberry Patch • Attn: Cookbook Dept.
PO Box 812 • Columbus, OH 43216-0812

* Don't forget to include your name, address, phone number and email address so we'll know how to reach you for your FREE book!

Find Gooseberry Patch
wherever you are!

www.gooseberrypatch.com

Call us toll-free at 1·800·854·6673

Grandma's aprons   creamy fudge

fluffy marshmallows

gifts for giving

warm gingerbread

homemade cocoa

buttercream frosting   cut-out cookies

U.S. to Metric Recipe Equivalents

Volume Measurements

1/4 teaspoon	1 mL
1/2 teaspoon	2 mL
1 teaspoon	5 mL
1 tablespoon = 3 teaspoons	15 mL
2 tablespoons = 1 fluid ounce	30 mL
1/4 cup	60 mL
1/3 cup	75 mL
1/2 cup = 4 fluid ounces	125 mL
1 cup = 8 fluid ounces	250 mL
2 cups = 1 pint =16 fluid ounces	500 mL
4 cups = 1 quart	1 L

Weights

1 ounce	30 g
4 ounces	120 g
8 ounces	225 g
16 ounces = 1 pound	450 g

Oven Temperatures

300° F	150° C
325° F	160° C
350° F	180° C
375° F	190° C
400° F	200° C
450° F	230° C

Baking Pan Sizes

Square

8x8x2 inches	2 L = 20x20x5 cm
9x9x2 inches	2.5 L = 23x23x5 cm

Rectangular

13x9x2 inches	3.5 L = 33x23x5 cm

Loaf

9x5x3 inches	2 L = 23x13x7 cm

Round

8x1-1/2 inches	1.2 L = 20x4 cm
9x1-1/2 inches	1.5 L = 23x4 cm